# UITAR *signature licks*

# THE **RED HOT CHILI PEPPERS**

## A Step-By-Step Breakdown of the Band's Guitar Styles and Techniques

### by Dale Turner

ISBN 0-7935-8049-8

# HAL•LEONARD®
## CORPORATION

7777 W. BLUEMOUND RD. P.O. BOX 13819 MILWAUKEE, WI 53213

Visit Hal Leonard Online at
**www.halleonard.com**

# THE RED HOT CHILI PEPPERS

## TABLE OF CONTENTS

# INTRODUCTION

Throughout their career, the Red Hot Chili Peppers have consistently been successful in fusing funk, punk, rap, and rock into a uniquely marketable hybrid, which countless fans view as the "alternative to the alternative." Each recorded effort by the Red Hot Chili Peppers has not only paved the way for other funk-oriented hardcore bands across the country (e.g., Fishbone, fIREHOSE, Living Colour, and Faith No More) but has documented the band's own continuing evolution, both as musicians and as distinctive personalities.

Since the formation of the Red Hot Chili Peppers in the spring of 1983 (originally called "Tony Flow and the Miraculously Majestic Masters of Mayhem"), the band has endured numerous changes in personnel. To date, the guitar chair has been held by no fewer than seven axe-wielders: Jack Sherman, Hillel Slovak (died June 27, 1988), Dewayne "Blackbyrd" McKnight, John Frusciante, Arik Marshall, Jesse Tobias (for about two weeks), and now, Dave Navarro (formerly of Jane's Addiction). In addition, drummer Chad Smith replaced Jack Irons who vacated the drum throne shortly after guitarist Hillel Slovak died. The Red Hot Chili Peppers' founding members, Anthony Kiedis and Flea (Michael Balzary), met in their teens at Fairfax High School in Los Angeles. Throughout triumph and tragedy, the pair have remained optimistic, with an unwavering intent on remaining firmly rooted in reason, despite having to live in a world that sometimes seems doomed by design—in fact, Flea and Ant once even admitted to jokingly discussing changing the band's name to "The Doom Prolongers."

If you're a Pepper fan, you've come to the right place! Proceed with caution as you flip through the following pages. You're about to be treated to a smorgasbord of funk, punk, rap, and rock riffs of doom—even a couple of the band's acoustic classics. Selections from *Freaky Styley*, *The Uplift Mofo Party Plan*, *Mother's Milk*, *BloodSugarSexMagik*, *One Hot Minute*, and a special soundtrack section have been included, bringing the song total to twelve tunes in all. Many of these songs have been mainstays in the Red Hot Chili Peppers' live set for years.

Remember, it takes more than practice to play like a Pepper. Their music reflects each band member's personal experience—the good, the bad, and the ugly. Take it from the band (as printed on the last page of the *One Hot Minute* CD booklet insert): "Through the years, the Red Hot Chili Peppers have roosted in the hen house and wallowed in the pig sty."

# THE RECORDING

The CD included with this book was recorded on a Roland VS-880V2 digital eight-track hard-disk recorder, using its internal VS8F-1 expansion board for all simulated amplifier tones (e.g., Matchless, Soldano, 5150, etc.), digital effects (chorus, delay, compression, etc.), and microphone enhancements. Two different Tom Anderson Strats were used to cover all electric guitar parts, while a Larivée six-string (equipped with a Highlander pickup) and a Taylor twelve-string were played for the acoustic songs. Both electric guitars were strung with D'Addario EXL110s, while the six-string acoustic featured D'Addario EJ17s. The drums were programmed onto an Alesis HR-16 drum machine, and a Yamaha BBN411 bass guitar was used to recreate all bass lines. All guitar, bass, and drums tracks were then mixed down to an Otari DTR-8S DAT recorder.

I would like to extend my thanks to Erik Hanson at Roland Corporation US, Greg Romano at J. D'Addario & Company, Inc. for the strings and picks, Derek Snyder and Craig Booker at West L.A. Music, Joe Jewell for lending me his Taylor twelve-string, and everybody at Hal Leonard Publishing Corporation.

# Freaky Styley

Though initially formed as a joke, the "Miraculously Majestic Masters of Mayhem" rechristened themselves the "Red Hot Chili Peppers" in 1984 (purportedly after Anthony Kiedis saw those words burning on a bush in the Hollywood hills while "tripping") and soon found themselves conquering the L.A. underground scene, becoming one of the most in-demand club acts in town. It didn't take long for record reps to notice them either. At that time, the band's lineup consisted of Anthony Kiedis, Flea, Hillel Slovak, and Jack Irons. It seemed that nothing could stop their unprecedented momentum—nothing except for the fact that Slovak and Irons were also in a band called "What Is This" with guitarist Alain Johannes.

When the Red Hot Chili Peppers were approached by EMI America for a seven-record deal, What Is This was also about to be signed—by MCA. Slovak and Irons had to make a decision about which band to stay with. They chose What Is This because they'd spent six years with the band—as opposed to the six *months* they'd spent with their "joke band." EMI gave the remaining Red Hot Chili Peppers only a few months to audition new members and fill out the band's roster. Anthony and Flea chose studio musician and guitarist Jack Sherman and drummer Cliff Martinez for the band's first album, *The Red Hot Chili Peppers*.

This first album was hardly an accurate portrayal of the intense energy and passion possessed by the Red Hot Chili Peppers, mostly because they were not in full force on the recording (obviously due to the absence of Slovak and Irons). The fact that producer (ex-Gang of Four guitarist) Andy Gill's primary objective was to create a hit record—in the tradition of MTV bands like Duran Duran, the Thompson Twins, Frankie Goes to Hollywood, etc.—didn't help matters either.

In January 1985, guitarist Jack Sherman got the boot. It was clear that he and the band just didn't "click" live or in the studio. Sherman and the band parted ways, free of any hostilities or bitterness. (He later performed background vocals on two songs which wound up on the *Mother's Milk* album in 1989—"Good Time Boys" and "Higher Ground.") Meanwhile, Hillel Slovak, who as of late hadn't been satisfied with the direction in which What Is This was heading, rejoined Anthony and Flea upon their request. Anthony Kiedis ("Homes"), Flea ("Homeboy"), Hillel Slovak ("Homesqueeze"), and Cliff Martinez ("Homey") soon got to work on creating their sophomore effort, *Freaky Styley*.

For their second time at bat, the Red Hot Chili Peppers requested George Clinton of Parliament/Funkadelic to fulfill the role as producer. (Flea had recently discovered Clinton's brand of '70s funk and freaked over it.) The Chilis went to Detroit to cut the album at Clinton's own United Sound Studio during the spring of 1985. They presented Clinton with a handful of raw riffs, melodies, and lyrics, and Clinton helped refine them. The end result was a product that oozed with sexy swank—complete with titles like "Lovin' and Touchin'" and "Sex Rap." "Catholic School Girls Rule" also made the cut, providing the band with one of what would soon be many crowd-pleasers.

The media neglected to give the band the attention it seemed to deserve, however, resulting in somewhat dismal returns in the record sales department. (The first two albums only sold about 75,000 apiece.) Needless to say, the Red Hot Chili Peppers were far from a household name. At this time, college radio and the "fraternity circuit" played a vital role in helping to establish the Peppers' fan base across the country, helping to spread the word of this local Los Angeles phenomenon beyond the boundaries of California.

In April 1986, missing his relationship with Hillel, Jack Irons rejoined the Red Hot Chili Peppers. Like Slovak a year earlier, Irons wasn't pleased with the direction that What Is This seemed to be headed. He also missed his Red Hot buddies.

# CATHOLIC SCHOOL GIRLS RULE

**Words and Music by Anthony Kiedis, Flea and Cliff Martinez**

"Catholic School Girls Rule," perhaps the most alluring track from *Freaky Styley*, unloads on listeners with its comical confessions of the Red Hot Chili Peppers' sexual obsessions and fixations. Accompanied by a video that MTV wouldn't touch with the proverbial ten-foot pole (it was released later on the RHCP video collection *Positive Mental Octopus*), this Chili Peppers classic depicts the band at its funky-punky best, spurting with the inimitable energy and angst of the late Hillel Slovak.

### Figure 1—Intro/Chorus

Hillel spices up this song's primary riff, which basically doubles Flea's bass line, by interjecting a handful of squealing *natural harmonics* every chance he gets. Natural harmonics occur on any stringed instrument (guitar, violin, harp, etc.) when one of its strings is lightly touched at a particular point. (In notation, harmonics are represented with diamond-shaped noteheads and the abbreviation "Harm." between the notation and TAB staves.) Throughout this intro/chorus section, harmonics are mostly performed in simultaneous groups of three or four. The first such group appears in measure 1 (on beat 3) and occurs across the fourth frets of strings 3–6. These notes sound exactly two octaves and a major third higher than their "fundamental" source, the "normal" pitches of the open strings.

To execute harmonics like those depicted in measure 1, lightly lay your first finger across the fourth fret (directly *over* the fret). Try to avoid pressing the strings down into the fretboard—all you want to do is *touch* the string. While your finger is laying there, pick the strings, then quickly remove your fret-hand finger. The result should be the production of four squealing pitches identical to those heard in your audio source!

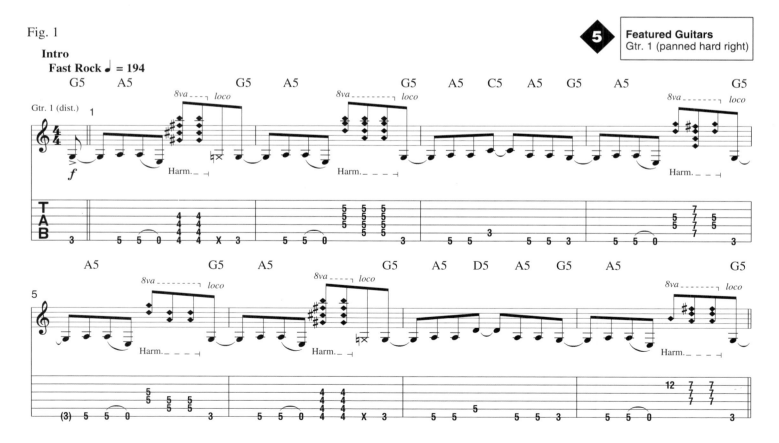

Fig. 1

**5** Featured Guitars
Gtr. 1 (panned hard right)

**Intro**
**Fast Rock** ♩ = 194

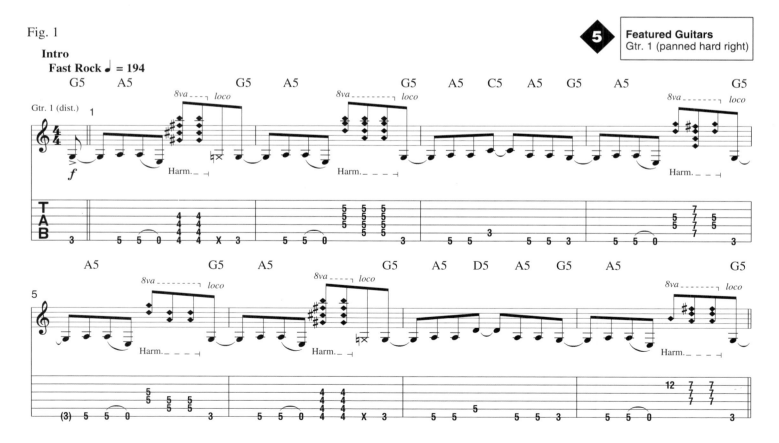

*Catholic school girls rule...*

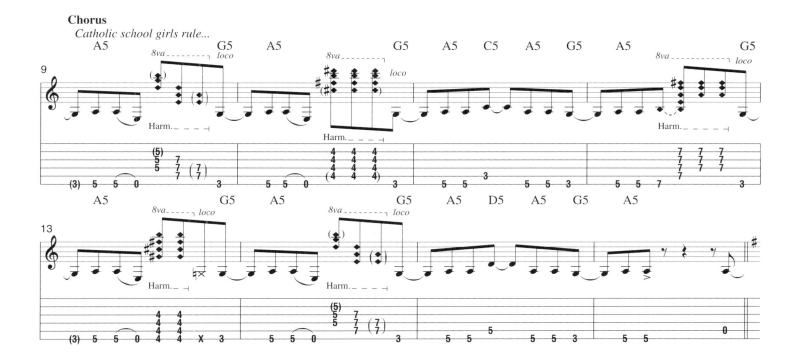

## Figure 2—First Verse

For the verse sections, the song shifts into a different mode (literally!)—B Phrygian (B–C–D–E–F♯–G–A). Hillel doubles Flea's bass line once again, only this time in just the odd-numbered measures (1, 3, 5, etc.). In every other measure (2, 4, 6, etc.) Hillel improvises with arpeggiated chordal fills (measure 4) and strummed chord figures (measure 6).

Fig. 2

**6** Featured Guitars
Gtr. 1 (panned hard right)

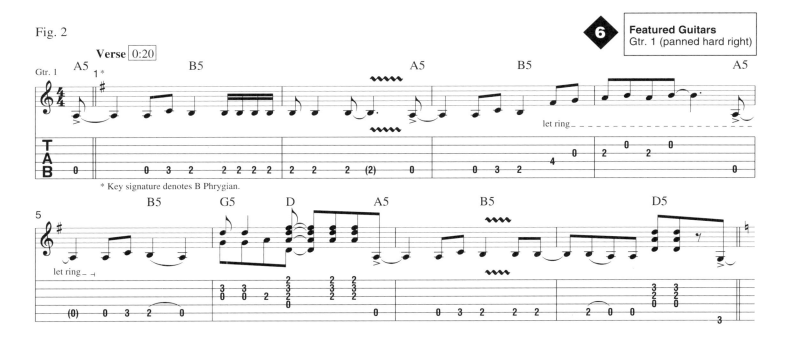

## Figure 3—Bridge

As things heat up in this tune, Hillel and Flea combine their strengths and perform the single-note bridge figure depicted in Figure 3 in perfect unison. Notice that the notes used throughout this syncopated line are confined strictly to the sixth string.

Fig. 3

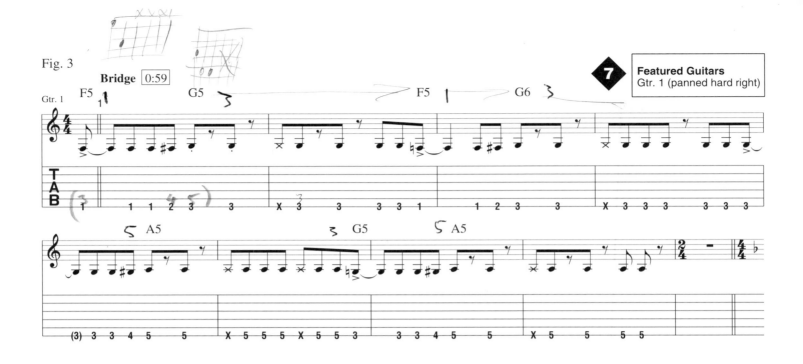

## Figure 4—Interlude

While Flea and Hillel (Gtr. 1) play a similar single-note figure in the key of D natural minor (D–E–F–G–A–B♭–C), an additional guitar (Gtr. 2) provides chord stabs on the "and" portion of beat 2 (measures 1, 2, 4, and 5). By measure 6, both guitars join forces and ride out this riff's remaining measures by aggressively smacking a fully-fretted E chord, which is performed in rhythmic unison with the bass and drums.

Fig. 4

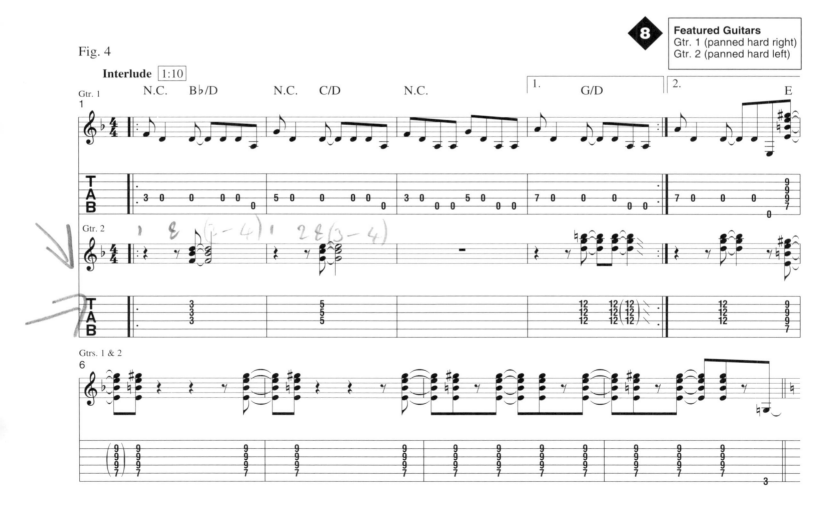

# The Uplift Mofo Party Plan

With the Red Hot Chili Peppers returned to full strength, it seemed that nothing could stop their rise to the top of the funk-punk-rap-rock ranks. Rap-rock bands like Run DMC and the Beastie Boys were hitting the charts, giving rap/rock fusion the exposure and respect it deserved. To give the Chili Peppers' a better chance at challenging the newly-found success of their rap-rock counterparts, EMI America transferred its responsibilities to the more functional EMI Manhattan—a branch of the same label that could be more in-touch and hands-on with RHCP.

Unfortunately, during this period, Anthony and Hillel were using heroin on a regular basis. (Hillel may have even been hooked as far back as 1984.) Before Jack rejoined the band, Flea had been a nervous wreck trying to deal with the escalating chemical intake of his buddies. Jack's return eased the tension for a bit, but it wasn't long before Hillel's pharmaceutical dabblings began to take their toll.

In January 1987, after months of being on the road, the Red Hot Chili Peppers entered Capitol Studios with Michael Beinhorn (the band chose him after interviewing several candidates) to begin preproduction for their third album. At the time, however, the Red Hot Chili Peppers only had five completed songs. Insufficient in Beinhorn's eyes, he decided he'd take it upon himself to oversee the band's lifestyle—keeping tabs on them and monitoring their work ethic. Beinhorn temporarily moved out of his home, relocated to the same block Anthony Kiedis lived, and basically *made* them work. The Chili Peppers didn't return to the studio until May 1987, but the end result was well worth all the sweat.

*The Uplift Mofo Party Plan* was released in September 1987 and was the first RHCP recording to accurately depict the primal energy and explosiveness the band demonstrated in their live shows. Unlike George Clinton, who never saw a Peppers' show prior to producing *Freaky Styley*, Beinhorn was well aware of the band's live vibe and made every effort to capture their spirit on vinyl. Sadly, the album still failed to get airplay. The Red Hot Chili Peppers pounded the road with Fishbone and Thelonious Monster in an effort to force-feed *The Uplift Mofo Party Plan* to the masses, tackling one city at a time. The rigorous roadwork did come with its rewards (the album slowly pushed its way up the *Billboard* album chart to #143), but Hillel was fighting a losing battle.

With the band set to embark on its first European tour, it became clear that they couldn't afford to have anything in their organization that might hold them back. Anthony, Flea, and Jack had been going to great lengths to keep their friend functional, but they just couldn't shoulder him anymore. At one point, Anthony was going to break the news to Hillel, but Fishbone's Angelo Moore discouraged him. Hillel joined them in their jaunt to Europe. It was during this tour that the Red Hot Chili Peppers shot the "cocks in socks" cover art for their *Abbey Road* EP—ironically the Beatles' final album, and the last for Hillel. Hillel Slovak died on June 27, 1988—two weeks after the band returned from its European tour. Jack Irons left the band shortly thereafter.

# FIGHT LIKE A BRAVE

**Words and Music by Flea, Anthony Kiedis,**
**Hillel Slovak and Jack Irons**

"Fight Like a Brave" was released as the first single and video from *The Uplift Mofo Party Plan* in October 1987 and also happens to be the first track on the record. The song was intended to inspirit individuals with low self-esteem, encouraging them to pick themselves up off the floor and view life through optimistic eyes.

"Fight Like a Brave" received critical praise from a number of rock journalists. As Steve Blush wrote in *The Paper*, "'Fight Like a Brave' is the perfect blend of Run DMC/Beastie Boys metal-rap and Parliament acid funk 'n' roll."

### Figure 1—Verse

Here's the song's primary figure, which is performed similarly throughout each verse and at the tail end of each chorus. This riff gets its crunchy character from the various *double stops* (two-note chord partials) Hillel inserts amidst a droning open fifth string. These double stops are all oriented around the fifth position and provide a bit of minor/major ambiguity, as the notes C ("flat" third or "lowered" third) and C♯ (major third) are juxtaposed throughout an A Mixolydian-sounding groove (A–B–C♯–D–E–F♯–G). This repeated four-measure passage is punctuated each time with G5 and D5 power chords in measure 4 (beats 3 and 4, respectively).

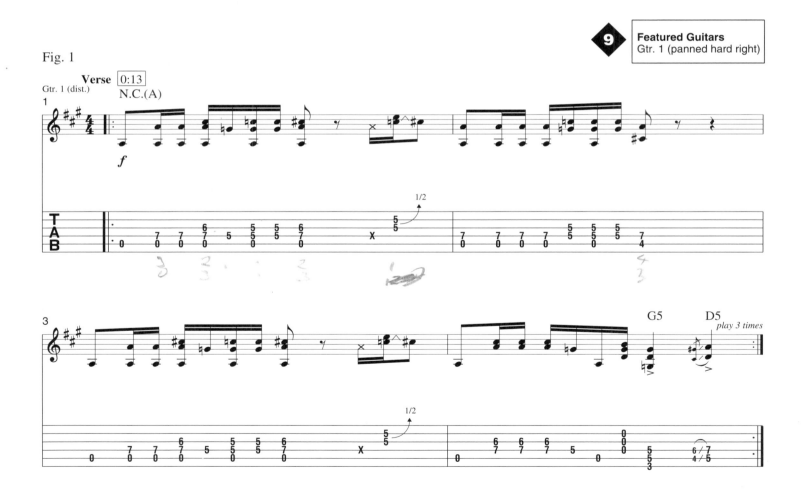

Fig. 1

9 Featured Guitars
Gtr. 1 (panned hard right)

**Figure 2—Chorus**

For the first four measures of this chorus riff, Hillel takes a figure that is reminiscent of the earlier verse sections, complete with similar double stops on beat 4 of measures 1 and 3, and *transposes* it up one whole step to the tonal area of B Mixolydian (B–C♯–D♯–E–F♯–G♯–A). "Transposition" occurs whenever a previously encountered melodic or harmonic idea is shifted verbatim to a new key area. By measure 5, the song's primary riff resumes in its original tonal area of A Mixolydian.

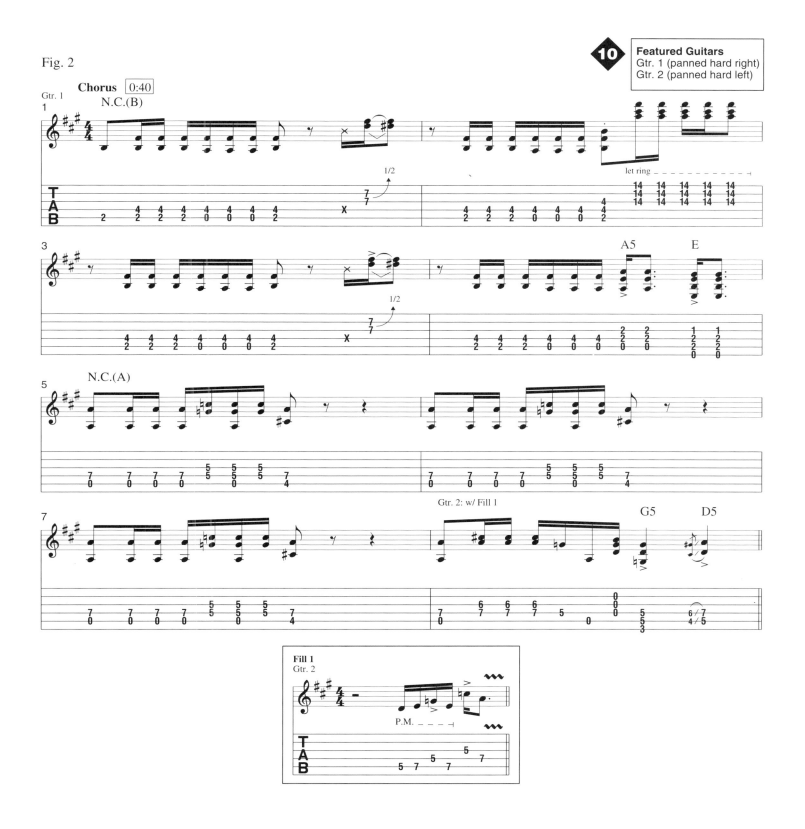

**Figure 3—Guitar Solo**

Hillel's approach towards recording this guitar solo yielded stunning results, as two guitars (panned hard left and hard right) are used to perform similar licks throughout. For the most part, just two different pentatonic scales are used in this note-fest, beginning with B minor pentatonic (B–D–E–F♯–A) in measures 1–2, then shifting to E minor pentatonic (E–G–A–B–D) for measures 3–6. By measure 7, both guitars split off from one another and engage in *harmonization*, borrowing notes from the E Dorian mode (E–F♯–G–A–B–C♯–D). "Harmonization" occurs whenever a melody played by one instrument is doubled by another instrument, but at a different pitch level. In the case of measures 7–9, Hillel harmonizes himself in *thirds*, playing the higher harmony notes (Gtr. 1) two scale tones higher than those found in the primary line (Gtr. 2). In measures 11–12, he opts to harmonize himself in *fifths*, playing the higher harmony notes four scale tones higher than the main melody.

As an effective climax to his solo, Hillel engages in a series of *pinch harmonics* in measure 11. "Pinch harmonics" are achieved by striking the indicated string with a downward pickstroke and allowing your pick-hand's thumb to come in contact with the string immediately afterward, on the "follow-through." If properly executed, an extra, squealing harmonic overtone (much higher in pitch) will be produced. With practice, you should be able to do this in one quick pick motion. If you can't get the appropriate pitches to squeak out, try attacking the string at a different point along its length. The closer you get to the bridge, the higher the pinch harmonic.

**Featured Guitars**
Gtr. 1 (panned hard left)
Gtr. 2 (panned hard right)

Fig. 3

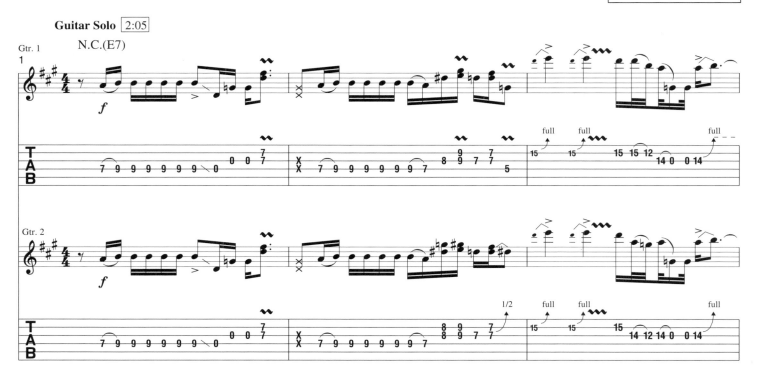

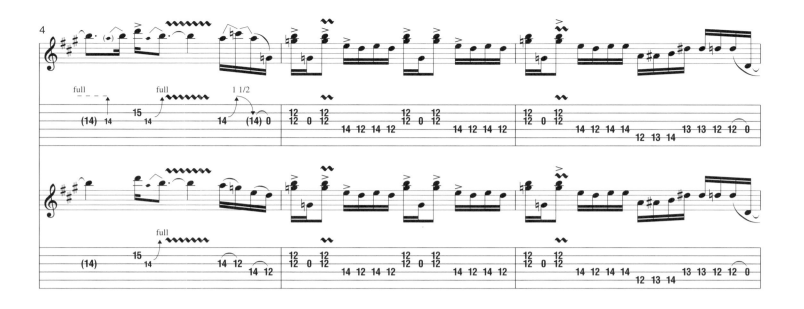

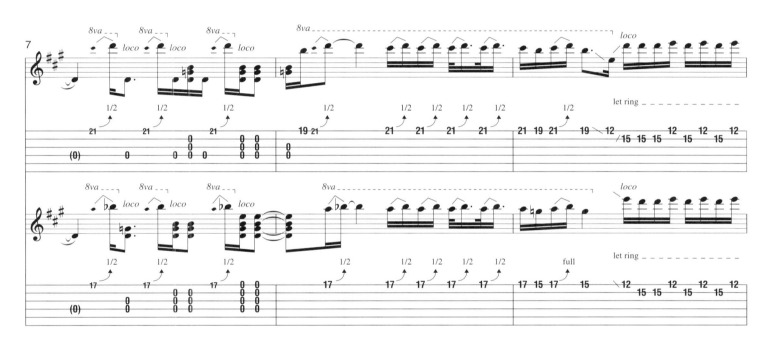

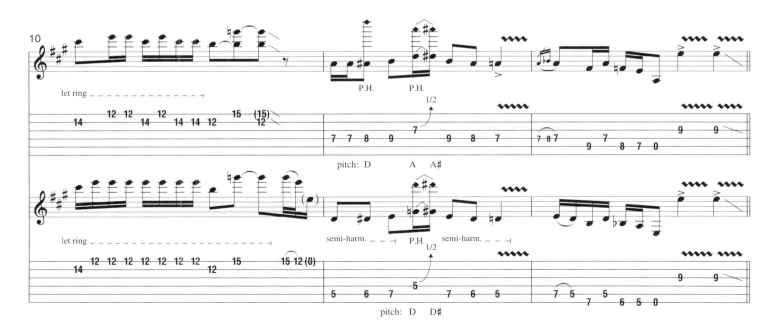

# Mother's Milk

With the death of Hillel came a change in the band's lifestyle. They became more focused on positive things like the basic loving bond between band members and no longer took those relationships for granted. Music and friendship would help navigate the band to the top. Hillel was replaced briefly by guitarist Dewayne "Blackbyrd" McKnight (he used to play with George Clinton in Parliament/Funkadelic) and D.H. Peligro (Dead Kennedys' drummer). However, the famed Chili Pepper magic didn't really return until John Frusciante entered the picture, replacing McKnight and making his debut with the Red Hot Chili Peppers at age 18. Frusciante's first appearance with the band was on a television show called *2HIP4TV*, which was broadcast on Christmas 1988.

When John Frusciante was growing up, he used to practice ten or fifteen hours a day, working on everything from technique and theoretical applications to Frank Zappa and Jimi Hendrix songs. The Red Hot Chili Peppers were Frusciante's favorite band in the world. He already knew all their guitar riffs, solos, lyrics, bass parts—everything. Flea, who met Frusciante through D.H. Peligro, had been recording some tunes at his house and invited him to come over and lay down some tracks. John's work was so impressive that Flea decided they'd better snatch him up right away. Shortly thereafter, Chad Smith replaced D.H. Peligro behind the drum kit. The newly-reformed Red Hot Chili Peppers hit the road in March 1989 to work out the new band's idiosyncrasies prior to recording their fourth album, *Mother's Milk*.

Produced by Michael Beinhorn, *Mother's Milk* (which Anthony referred to throughout its recording process as *Rocking Freakapotamus* before arriving at the current title) depicts a monstrous step in the Red Hot Chili Peppers' evolution—both as songwriters and as distinct musical personalities. The album was released in August 1989 and, as a tribute, featured cover art (back cover) by the late Hillel Slovak.

*Mother's Milk* was received by the media and the public with open arms. Words of praise spouted from the pens of rock journalists in magazines and newspapers across the country. In *Guitar Player* magazine, Joe Gore praised the guitar skills and creative genius of John Frusciante, stating that "[He] plays as if he grew up with one ear glued to a boombox and the other to a Marshall stack... a living archive of '70s metal and funk riffs." He went on to characterize the Chili Peppers' latest lineup as "the most intense yet." *Mother's Milk* went gold (500,000 copies sold) in April 1990.

# GOOD TIME BOYS

**Words and Music by Anthony Kiedis, Flea,
John Frusciante and Chad Smith**

"Good Time Boys" is the opening track off *Mother's Milk* and features some masterful riffery—courtesy of newcomer John Frusciante and his black Les Paul (blasted through a Soldano head)—as well as gang-style background vocals sung by, among others, ex-guitarist Jack Sherman (the first guitarist to record with RHCP).

"Good Time Boys" encapsulates the mentality of the Red Hot Chili Peppers of old (prior to Hillel's death), illustrating their early, arguably irresponsible partying days, while at the same time immortalizing the mid-eighties L.A. club scene in song. It was during this crucial period of the Peppers' development that other local bands like fIREHOSE, Fishbone, and Thelonious Monster started making big waves of their own.

### Figure 1—Intro

While John wanks on his whammy bar (Gtr. 2), yanking the pitch of a screeching harmonic all over the place in a spectacular display of *vibrato bar pitch bends/dives*, Gtr. 1 grinds along in the background with one of the song's primary riffs (measures 1–4). Note that Gtr. 1 is run through an activated wah-wah pedal, set in the treble position and used strictly as a tone filter (not oscillated back and forth).

A "vibrato bar pitch bend/dive" (Gtr. 2) appears in notation in a manner similar to a standard fret-hand pitch bend—with a pointed slur illustrating the fluctuation between pitches in notation. However, to specify that the bar is used for the pitch bend or dive, "w/bar" is indicated between the notation and TAB staves. A downward-sloping line indicates that the pitch of the note is to be lowered (depress the bar), while an upward-sloping line would indicate that the pitch is to be raised (pull up on bar). The amount the pitch shifts as a result of this action is indicated either above or below the TAB staff with a "-" or "+."

By measure 5, both Gtrs. 1 and 2 double up on the same riff, performing sixteenth notes in the open position. For the most part, this figure revolves around pitches borrowed from E minor pentatonic (E–G–A–B–D), with the occasional addition of C♯ (second fret, second string), alluding to the E Dorian mode (E–F♯–G–A–B–C♯–D), and a chromatic passing tone A♯/B♭ (first fret, fifth string). If you've seen the band play this song live (check out their *Psychedelic Sexfunk Live from Heaven* video, which features footage from the *Mother's Milk* tour), you may have noticed that John uses *strict downstrokes* on all the single-note lines throughout this passage. Not only does this help generate this riff's percussively choppy attack sound, it also aids in keeping things rhythmically tight. All throughout this section (measures 5–12), an additional guitar (Gtr. 3) bangs out E7♯9 and A chords (w/clean tone).

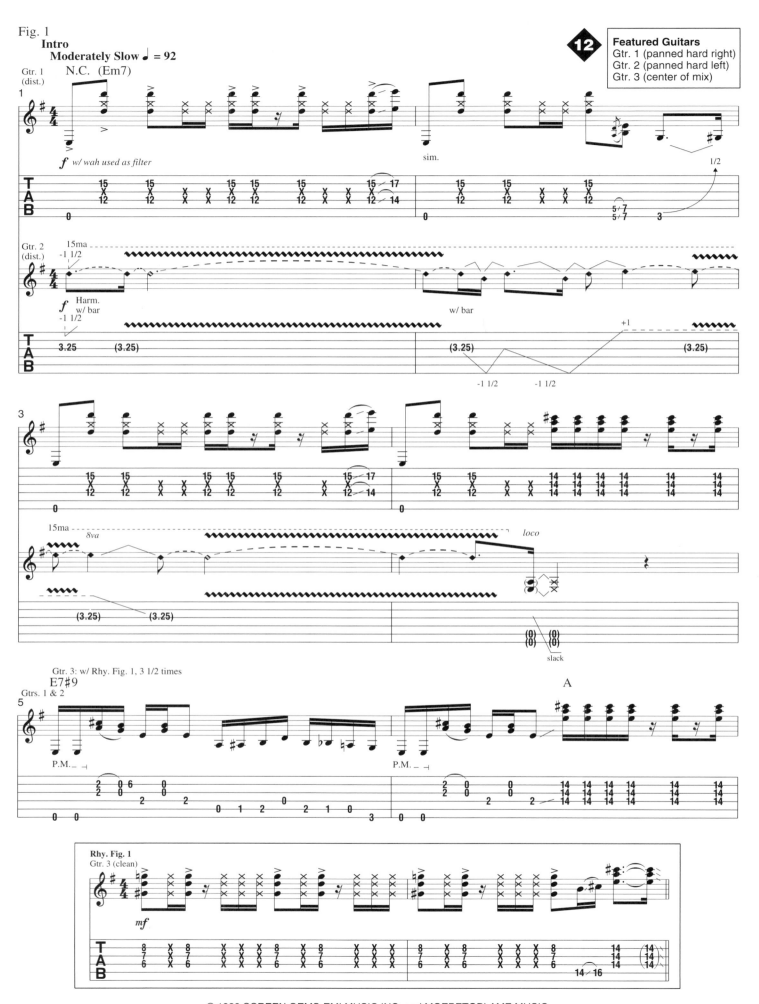

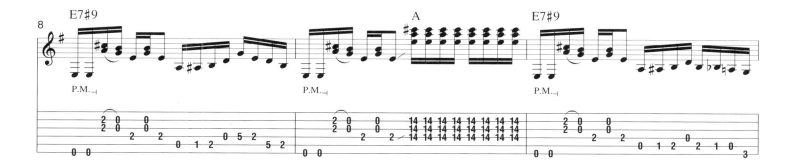

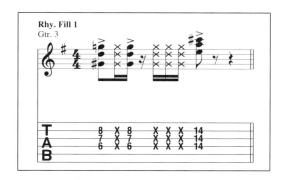

## Figure 2—Verse

This section features two highly-contrasting guitar parts—Gtrs. 1 and 2 perform brief bursts of distorted guitar phrases (measures 1-4 and 9-12), while Gtr. 3 funks out with a riff involving E7#9 chords and single notes confined to the third and fourth strings. By measure 5, Gtrs. 1 and 2 engage in a figure similar to Flea's bass line, alternating between the notes D and E  amidst punctuating double stops (measures 5–8).

In measure 12, John uses an effective half-step bend from A (second fret, third string) to B♭. This bend is also used in conjunction with a stationary note, D (third fret, second string), which is faded into courtesy of John's volume knob on the "and" portion of beat 3. This bending lick has maximum impact as it seems to come out of nowhere, preceded by complete silence since the band had ceased to play after beat 1. To hammer home the jarring effect of this musical moment, Flea also snaps out the note B♭ on his bass.

Fig. 2

**Verse** 0:32

E7#9

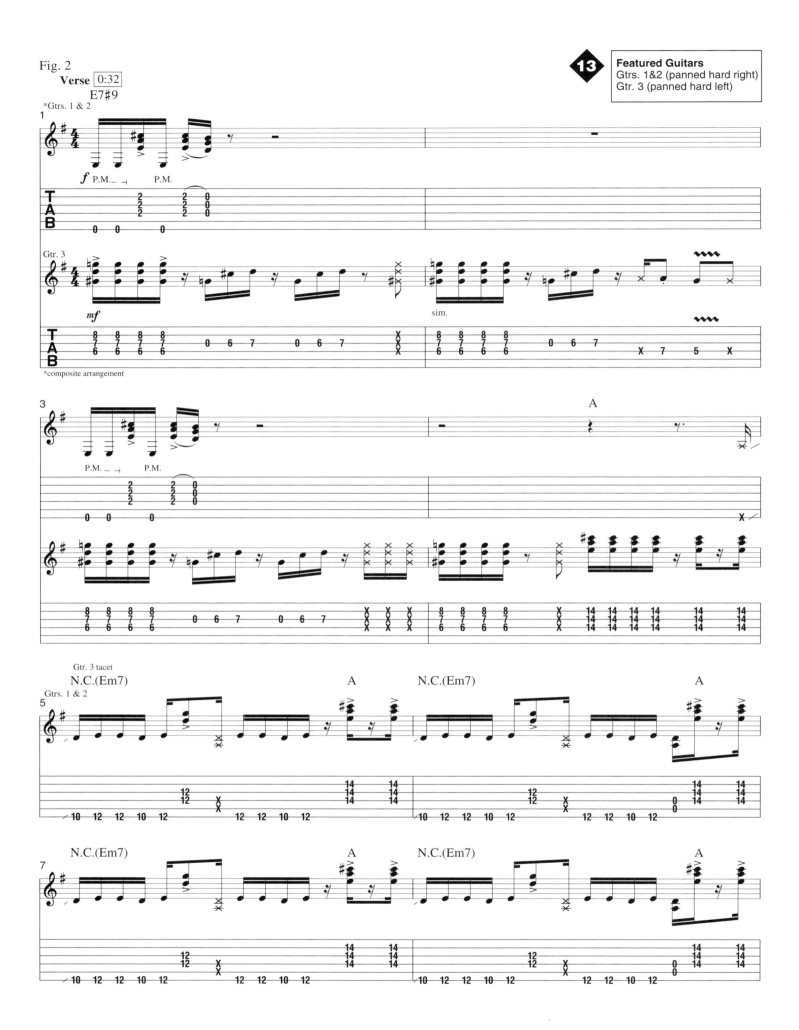

## Figure 3—Chorus

For this song's chorus figure, the band shifts briefly to the key of B minor while John proceeds to run through a handful of *double stops*, implying the chords Bm7, D5, and E5 with two-note chord partials. A "double stop" occurs whenever two notes are played simultaneously, often providing that little extra funky flavor that makes certain riffs sound magical. Probably one of hippest types of double-stop riffs around is the one-finger variety that John plays during the first half of measures 1 and 3 after the B5 chord, using his fourth finger to barre across the tenth fret of the top two strings to grab the notes A and D. These two notes are borrowed from the B natural minor scale (B–C♯–D–E–F♯–G–A) and, when heard in conjunction with B5 chord (B–F♯) on beat 1, imply the chord Bm7 (B–D–F♯–A).

After the band switches back to the key E minor in measures 5–8, John pulls out all the technical stops and plays a single-note riff reminiscent of the song's primary riff but with the addition of tricky intervallic licks and legato slides, slithering in and out of notes from E Dorian (E–F♯–G–A–B–C♯–D).

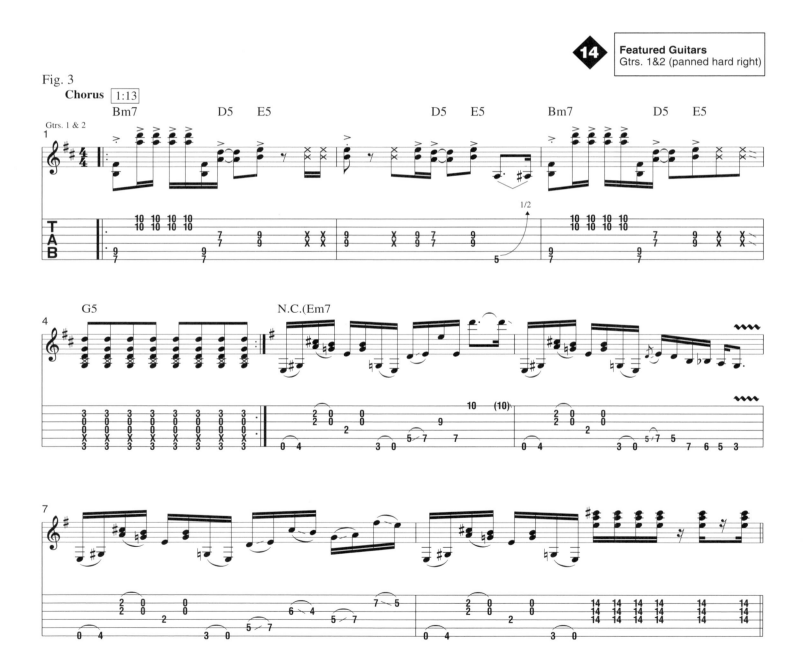

## Figure 4—Interlude

John and Flea create a massive wall of sound with this blistering single-note figure, which is tripled in three different octaves by Gtr. 1, Gtr. 2, and electric bass. Once again the band shifts keys, opting to perform this note-fest in G Dorian (G–A–B♭–C–D–E–F). Notice that Gtrs. 1 and 2 utilize the exact same fingering to perform each of their respective parts, but Gtr. 2 frets its notes exactly twelve frets (one octave) higher. As a means of punctuating this passage in measure 5, Gtr. 1 pulls off to its open sixth string and dive-bombs, slackening the low E string until it flaps across the pickups ("slack") after depressing the tremolo bar to the max. At the last possible moment, John grabs a squealing pinch harmonic way up at the nineteenth fret in a ferocious display of guitar noise effects.

**Figure 5—Outro Guitar Solo**

John puts the capper on this tune with this raunchy solo, using everything from orthodox bends, hammer-ons/pull-offs, and legato slides to unorthodox rakes (measure 2), bend-and-tap techniques (measure 6), and vibrato-bar bends (measure 7). If your fingers have flapped in a frenzy in the past, you may be sufficiently prepared to pluck through at least part of John's frantic demonstration of his pentatonic prowess. However, some of the more unorthodox techniques that pop up in this solo should probably be discussed first.

A technique that many outstanding guitar soloists engage in when they wish to give a note (or notes) that little extra snappy grit is called *raking*. This technique is used twice in this solo—first in measure 2 (beat 3) and second in measure 5 (beat 1). To properly execute a rake, all you need to do is lead into your targeted note by slicing your pick (with a downstroke) through the indicated strings, fretting the correct grace notes (indicated by smaller upstemmed notes in notation) with your index finger, in this case.

In measure 6, while holding a previous bend that was performed from the note A (second fret, third string) bent up one whole step to B, John quickly positions his pick hand over the fretboard and uses the second finger (middle) of this hand to "tap" onto the twelfth fret of the third string in a masterful demonstration of *bend and tap-on technique.* To execute a tap with your pick-hand finger, you must perform a technique that resembles the hammer-on. Here, instead of articulating a pitch on a string by slamming down a fret-hand finger onto the neck, you'll take a finger from your pick hand and slam it onto a fret indicated in TAB, producing the corresponding pitch in the notation. This technique is indicated over the notation staff with "+" and over the TAB staff as "T" (for "tap"). Since the tap here is used in conjunction with a note that is already bent one whole step, the resulting pitch will be one whole step higher than the note that normally occurs at the fret you're tapping on. Typically, the note on the twelfth fret of the third string is G. Since the earlier bend executed by the fret hand has already raised the pitch of the third string by one whole step, a tap on the twelfth fret will produce the note A.

Moments before Gtr. 1, Gtr. 2, and the electric bass engage in a riff reminiscent of the earlier interlude figure, John performs an extremely wide bend in measure 7 (beat 2) that tests the limits of his second string's snap potential! After bending the note E (seventeenth fret, second string) up one whole step to F♯, he yanks up on his vibrato bar to increase the pitch of the bend by an additional three whole steps! Ouch...

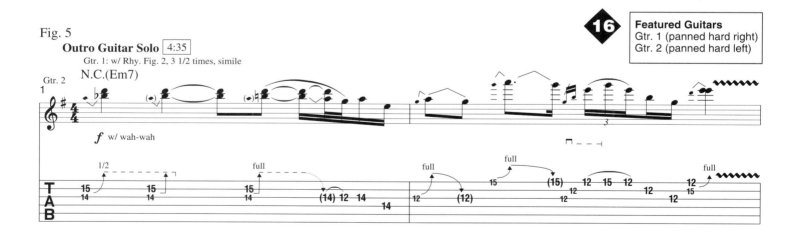

Fig. 5
**Outro Guitar Solo** 4:35

**16**

**Featured Guitars**
Gtr. 1 (panned hard right)
Gtr. 2 (panned hard left)

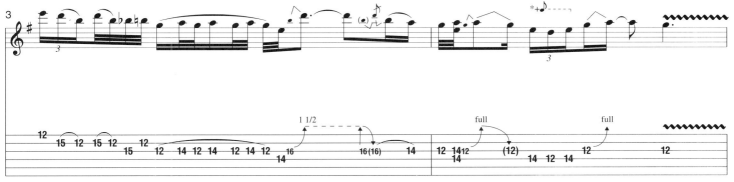

*Played slightly ahead of the beat.

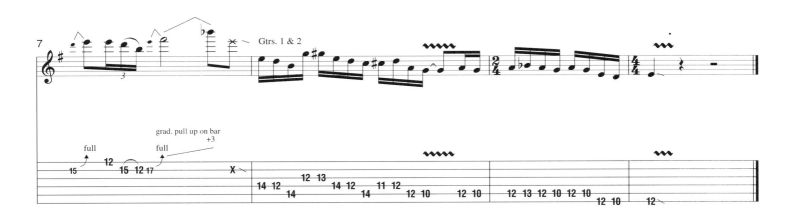

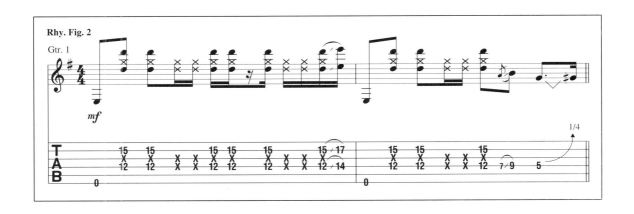

# SUBWAY TO VENUS

**Words and Music by Flea, Anthony Kiedis,
Chad Smith and John Frusciante**

Though never released as a single, "Subway to Venus" was a key component of the Chili Peppers' live set during the *Mother's Milk* tour. The song features some tricky ensemble figures and dazzling interplay between Flea and John Frusciante.

### Figure 1—Intro

If there was ever a tune that provided guitarists with a perfect vehicle for perfecting their *scratch rhythm* guitar chops, "Subway to Venus" is it! "Scratch rhythm" is a term derived from the "scratchy" sound that's produced when muted strings (the result of gently laying your fret-hand fingers across the guitar's strings without producing a discernable pitch) are strummed rhythmically with a pick, using a consistent down/up strumming motion. As you can see, this tune is full of rhythmic scratching. To get a handle on the technique, you may wish to begin practicing measure 4 first, as it involves playing steady sixteenth notes in a situation where the fret-hand fingers don't have to move. While maintaining a steady down/up strumming motion (beginning with a downstroke), practice this figure slowly several times until you can comfortably make the necessary timing adjustments between striking the accented (">") D octave figure, and striking the unaccented muted notes ("X"). Gradually increase your speed once you get things synchronized.

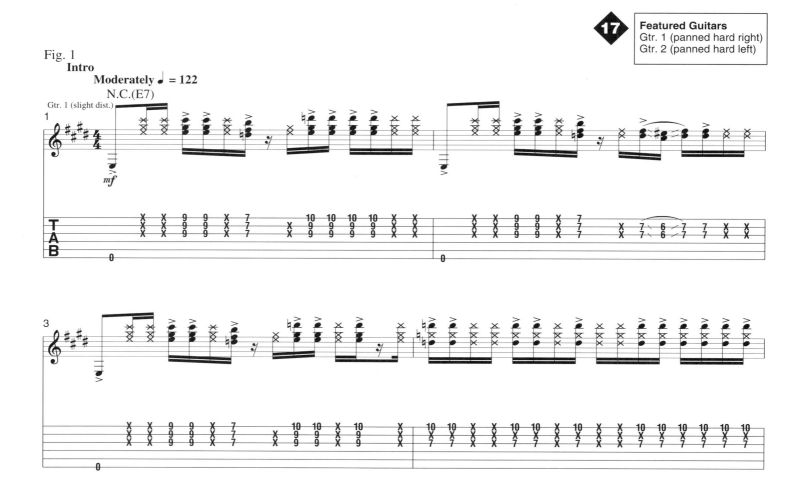

**17** **Featured Guitars**
Gtr. 1 (panned hard right)
Gtr. 2 (panned hard left)

Fig. 1
**Intro**
Moderately ♩ = 122
N.C.(E7)

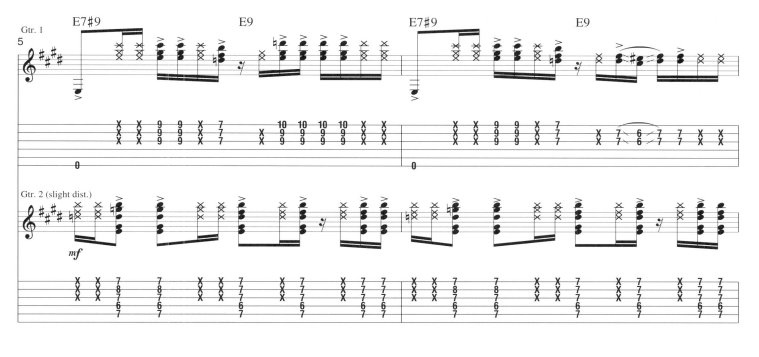

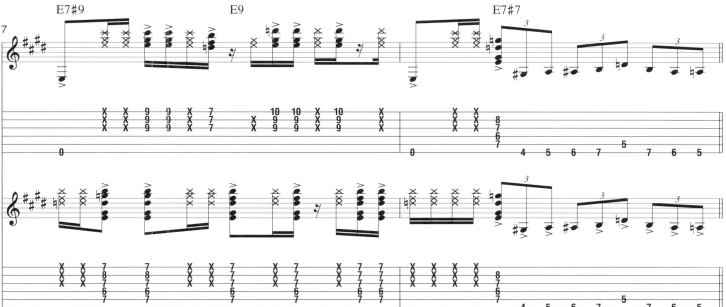

## Figure 2—First Verse

Here's an even better example of scratch rhythm guitar in action! Frusciante funks up a storm in this verse figure, holding down a chord fingering that rapidly fluctuates between E7#9 and E9 amidst relentless sixteenth-notes strums (Gtr. 1, measures 1–8). So that you may alternate between these two chords in the most efficient manner, try flattening out your third finger across the top three strings at the seventh fret when grabbing the E7#9 chord, using your fourth finger to fret the G (eighth fret, second string). By keeping your third finger barred across the seventh fret, all you need to do in order to make the transition between E7#9 and E9 is lift off your fourth finger. The A7#9 chords performed by Gtr. 2 in measures 9–11 and the initial entrance of Gtr. 2 back in Figure 1 (measures 5–7) also depict a similar, though less-manic, figure.

While Gtr. 2 engages in its own showcase of scratch rhythm playing in measures 9–11, Gtr. 1 opts for a single-note approach, playing syncopated funk lines rooted in A minor pentatonic at the fifth position. This section is punctuated with both guitars strumming two different inversions of a D7 chord (measure 12). A figure reminiscent of the song's earlier introduction immediately follows (measures 13–16).

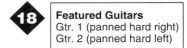

**Featured Guitars**
Gtr. 1 (panned hard right)
Gtr. 2 (panned hard left)

Fig. 2

**Verse** 0:16

26

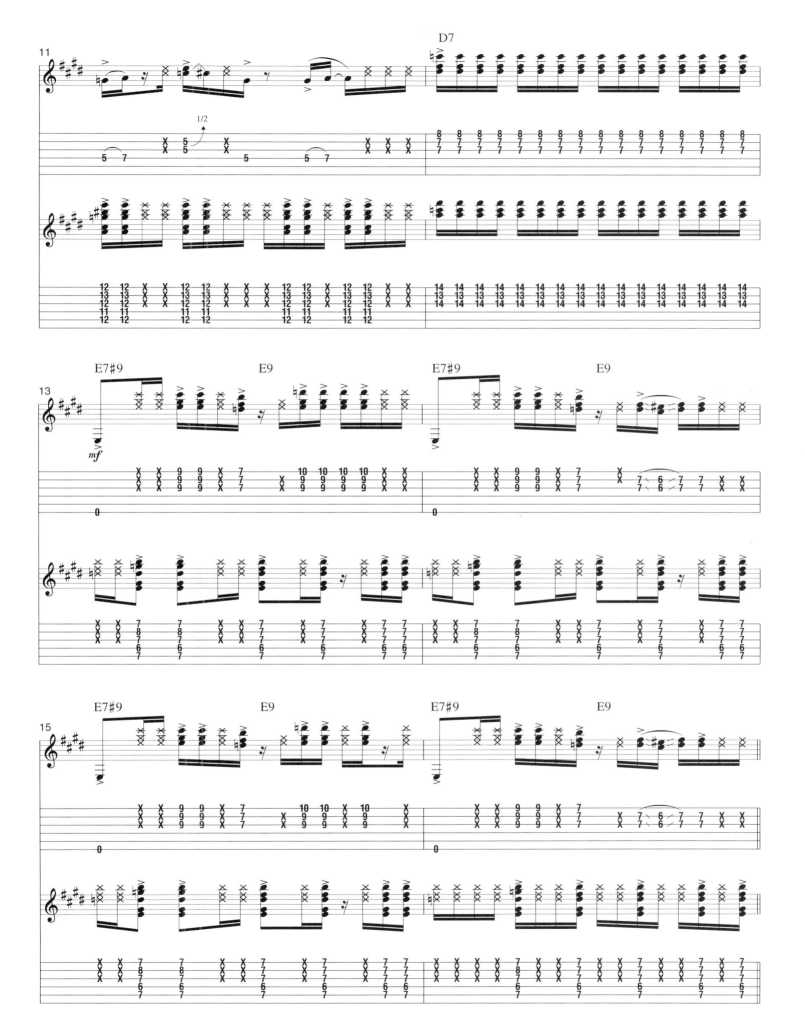

## Figure 3—Chorus

In this song's chorus riff, John takes a "call and response" approach towards orchestrating Gtrs. 1 and 2. While Gtr. 1 primarily doubles Flea's bass line (the primary figure, or "call"), Gtr. 2 performs double stops and rhythmic scratches between the musical cracks (the "response").

**19** Featured Guitars
Gtr. 1 (panned hard right)
Gtr. 2 (panned hard left)

*Double tracked at this point.

### Figure 4—Outro Guitar Solo

Over the course of this well-crafted, in-your-face solo section, multiple guitars are used to achieve an intense mass of musical madness! Gtrs. 1 and 2 start things rolling, performing a D octave shape in a manner similar to what we explored in measure 4 of this song's introduction. After four repetitions of this figure, both guitars barre across the twelfth fret of strings 2–4 and start funking out (Rhy. Fig. 1). Meanwhile, Gtr. 3 enters, doubling Flea's bass line (Riff A). By measure 3, John pulls out all the stops, blasting yet another guitar (Gtr. 4) over the top of this constantly-evolving soundscape.

Gtr. 4 makes its initial statement by playing a descending sequence of *unison bends* in measures 3–4. A "unison" occurs whenever two identical pitches in the same octave are performed simultaneously. In a "unison bend," a note is fretted on one string, while a note from a lower adjacent string is played simultaneously and bent up to the same pitch. On beat 1 of measure 3, John *screams* with a unison bend consisting of two different B notes, playing one on the second string at the twelfth fret, and matching its pitch by way of a whole-step bend from the note A found at the fourteenth fret of the third string. This pair of B notes resonates in a different way than a single B would. This is due in large part to the intense finger vibrato John applies to the fretted B on the third string. The fluctuation in pitch generated from his vibrato creates a terrifying sound (not unlike the sound of an amp's speaker being ripped apart) as it is heard in conjunction with the unwavering pitch of the stationary B note on the second string. John takes this same unison bend shape and moves it down the fretboard, grabbing notes from E Dorian along the way (E–F#–G–A–B–C#–D). He concludes the first four measures of his lead statement with an open-position E minor pentatonic (E–G–A–B–D) outburst, manipulating open strings and other notes with his whammy bar (measures 5–6).

Measures 7–8 depict John at his most dazzling, ripping through a sequence of descending octave intervals in measure 7—all in E minor pentatonic! Just when you think it couldn't get any scarier, John follows up this frightening lick with a rapid series of hammer-ons, snaking his fingers down the fretboard through several different pentatonic positions until he arrives at the open position at the beginning of measure 9. The song is effectively climaxed after Gtrs. 2 and 4 lay out ("tacet") and the remaining guitars bang out power chords in synchronization with Flea's bass work and Chad's skin pounding (measure 11).

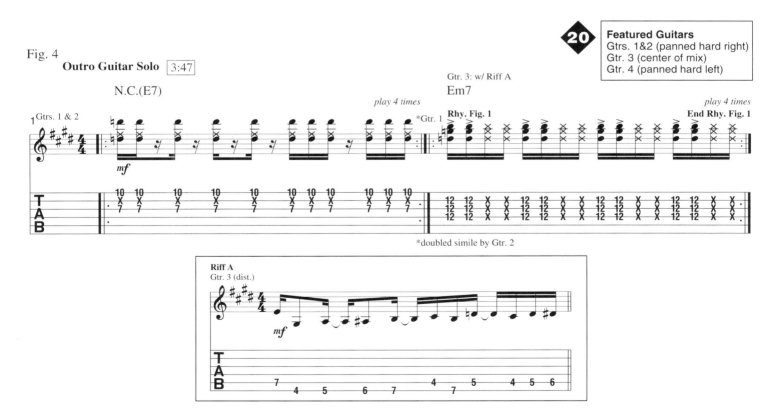

**Featured Guitars**
Gtrs. 1&2 (panned hard right)
Gtr. 3 (center of mix)
Gtr. 4 (panned hard left)

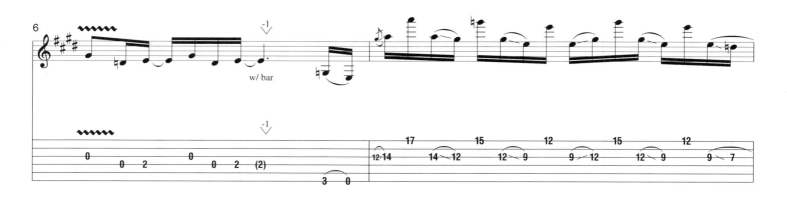

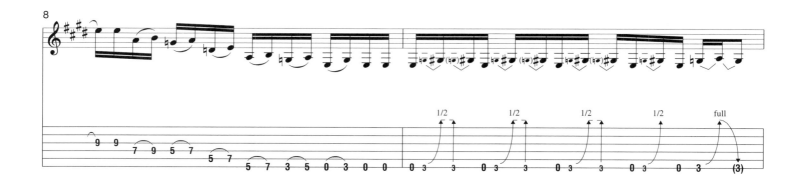

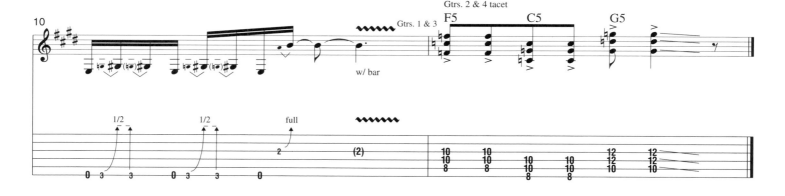

# TASTE THE PAIN

**Words and Music by Flea, Anthony Kiedis,
John Frusciante and Darren Henley**

"Taste the Pain" was originally recorded for the *Say Anything* soundtrack with Fishbone's drummer, Fish, pounding the skins. (Chad Smith wasn't in the Chili Peppers at the time of the recording.) Released as the third single from *Mother's Milk* in February of 1990, "Taste the Pain" illustrates the nocturnal lifestyle of a love-sick insomniac.

### Figure 1—Verses

In this verse riff, John uses a pair of guitars (Gtr. 2 played third and fourth verses only) to create a captivating background figure behind Anthony's riveting vocal. While rocking back and forth on his wah-wah pedal in steady quarter notes (Gtr. 1), John grabs single notes and double stops in a syncopated sixteenth-note riff derived from the E Dorian mode (E–F#–G–A–B–C#–D). To firmly outline the chord changes implied by a combination of Flea's bass line and the double stops performed by Gtr. 1, an additional guitar (Gtr. 2) is used on beats 2 and 4 to reinforce the harmonic shift between Em7 (measures 1 and 3) and A9 (measures 2 and 4).

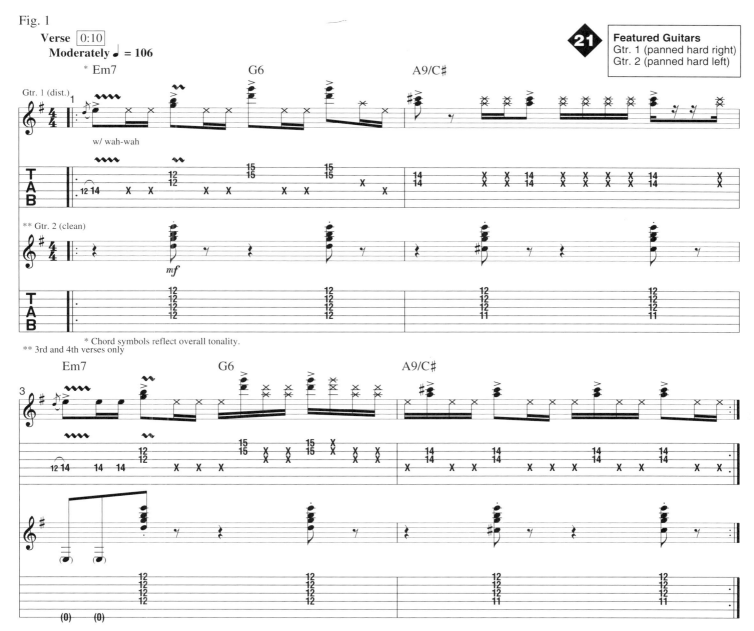

## Figure 2—Chorus

Once again, funky Frusciante creatively orchestrates a pair of guitars, this time in the context of a chorus riff. While Gtr. 3 (w/dist.) doubles Flea's bass line, Gtr. 1 discontinues its wah-wah effect and opts for a clean tone, performing a combination of E7#9, Am, and Em chords over the course of a repeated two-measure phrase.

**Featured Guitars**
Gtr. 1 (panned hard right)
Gtr. 3 (panned hard left)

Fig. 2

# BloodSugarSexMagik

Though *Mother's Milk* achieved gold-record status, there was widespread doubt within the Red Hot Chili Peppers organization that their current label, EMI Manhattan, would be able to commit the necessary resources to successfully market another Chili Peppers album. It was the band's belief that, in more competent hands, *Mother's Milk* could have easily gone platinum (1,000,000 copies sold). Almost instantly, the band found itself being courted by a handful of major record labels like MCA, Virgin, Def American (Rick Rubin's label), and Geffen, among many others, but it was Sony that came in with the highest bid—a three-record deal for approximately $5.7 million. The band decided that this was more than enough to bring an end to the bidding war. That evening, however, Warner Brothers' president, Mo Ostin, personally telephoned each member of the Red Hot Chili Peppers one at a time at their individual homes, congratulating them on their deal with Sony. Mr. Ostin wished the band all the luck in the world. The human element demonstrated by Ostin had such a profound effect on each band member that they all agreed to sign with Warner Brothers instead of Sony—reportedly a three-record deal for $10 million.

Rick Rubin would be the producer for the Red Hot Chili Peppers' first album with Warner Brothers. Known for his work with Run DMC, the Beastie Boys, and Public Enemy, Rubin had a knack for creating the perfect creative environment to suit any of his clients' practical and/or inspirational needs. In an effort to maximize the Chili Peppers' energies and help them maintain focus, Rubin decided that the best thing for the band would be to isolate them from the general population as much as possible. So that they'd be free from everyday distractions, Rubin put them up in a gargantuan Hollywood Hills mansion which, among many missing modern amenities, didn't even have a functioning telephone. It was here that the Chili Peppers would record their breakthrough album, *BloodSugarSexMagik*.

Rubin loaded all of his recording gear into the basement of the house, bringing nothing with him but the bare essentials. The band would record all of the album's basic tracks live with minimal overdubs. As it turns out, John Frusciante didn't even need that luxury; he cut most of his guitar solos live while recording the basic tracks. All totaled, the Red Hot Chili Peppers recorded twenty-four songs at their rented residence in just eight weeks—seventeen of which made it onto the record. Some that didn't make the final cut include "Fela's Cock" (an instrumental), "Sikamikanico," and some covers—two Hendrix songs ("Castles Made of Sand" and "Little Miss Lover") and an Iggy and the Stooges tune ("Search and Destroy"). The band's long-awaited blockbuster, *BloodSugarSexMagik*, was released in September 1991, stayed in the Top 10 for over a year, and quickly went triple platinum.

Unfortunately, the tour in support of *BloodSugarSexMagik* (RHCP toured with Pearl Jam and the Smashing Pumpkins, who were later replaced by Nirvana) proved to be the final straw that broke John Frusciante's back. John quickly grew weary of playing the multiple monstrous venues, missing the intimacy and interaction that smaller audiences provided. Frusciante jumped ship in May of 1992 while the *BloodSugarSexMagik* tour passed through Japan. Guitarless, the Chili Peppers had to cancel their tour. Though Dave Navarro (formerly of Jane's Addiction) was the first on the band's list as replacement guitarist, he reportedly refused because the approaching Lollapalooza II tour (which had booked the Chili Peppers) would put him too close to the event's organizer—former Jane's Addiction frontman, Perry Farrell. (Jane's Addiction disbanded at the conclusion of the first Lollapalooza tour in 1990.) Picking his own brain for an alternate, Flea remembered a guy he had played with two years ago in an instrumental funk outfit called Trulio Disgracias. The guitarist's name was Arik Marshall. Three-and-a-half weeks later, Arik was in Belgium with the Red Hot Chili Peppers playing in front of 60,000 people—the first of many shows the band would perform during their Lollapalooza II tour.

# BREAKING THE GIRL

**Words and Music by Anthony Kiedis, Flea,
Chad Smith and John Frusciante**

"Breaking the Girl" was released as the fourth single from *BloodSugarSexMagik* in June of 1992 and demonstrated a subtler side of the Red Hot Chili Peppers. Dominated by John Frusciante's acoustic twelve-string guitar textures, this Beatlesque pop hit helped pave the way for upcoming acoustic-based favorites like "My Friends" from *One Hot Minute*.

### Figure 1—Intro/Verses

Figure 1 depicts this song's intro/verse strumming riff, which is repeated similarly throughout both sections. Make sure that you've tuned all the strings of your acoustic guitar down one half step (a popular *slack tuning* used by rockers ranging from Hendrix to Nirvana) before you tackle this one—especially if you plan on jamming along with the recording. Track 3 on the accompanying CD should help you detune your instrument to the appropriate pitches.

You'll probably find that the trickiest part of this four-measure passage is Frusciante's syncopated strumming pattern. To help with this, try synchronizing your picking hand to the counting pattern below (between the notation and TAB staves) and using consistent down-up strumming, beginning with a downstroke. Every instance a chord is supposed to be strummed, the corresponding syllable in the counting pattern is italicized ("*one*-and, *two*-and, *three*-and, *four*-and, *five*-and, *six*-and," etc.). Once you've locked into this rhythmic groove, all you need to do is move the triad shape (fretted notes on strings 2–4) up to the indicated frets and apply the same strumming pattern in each of the remaining measures.

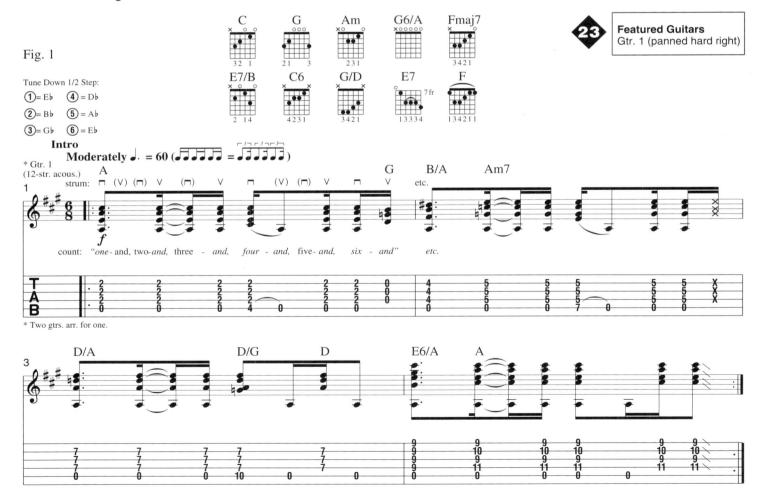

## Figure 2—Pre-Chorus

This pre-chorus figure, presented in *slash notation*, is based on a handful of open-position chords you probably learned in your first guitar lesson! Don't get spooked by the G6/A chord that occurs on the last beat (beat 6) of measure 3—if you look back at the chord frames at the beginning of Figure 1, you'll see that this chord name is just a fancy way of analyzing the sound produced by the simultaneous sounding of the top five open strings. While shifting between chords, many guitarists will opt to simply smack their instrument's open strings as a means of keeping the groove going, providing them with an extra split second to reposition their fingers so they can easily make the transition to the next chord.

## Figure 3—Chorus

This arrangement of chords was generated by an ascending bass line that begins with the note A (open fifth string) and continues in a scalar fashion all the way up to E (seventh fret, fifth string). You may find that some of the voicings John grabs are pretty tricky, particularly E7/B and C6, so be patient with yourself. Remember, John practiced this stuff (and a million other things) ten to fifteen hours a day!

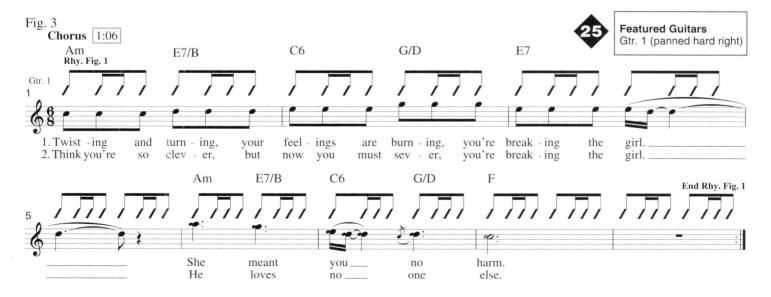

## Figure 4—Interlude

For the curious, this industrialized, percussive interlude section was inspired by and performed on a mess of hub caps, trash cans, and steel pipes that littered the lobby of the Hollywood Hills mansion the Chili Peppers resided/recorded at during the making of *BloodSugarSexMagik*. After recording the basic tracks for this song, each band member sat in a circle and pounded their hearts out on assigned pieces of hardware, laying down the aggressive groove heard on the classic album version (programmed on a drum machine for this instructional recording). In John's guitar part below, portions of the figure are performed with accents (indicated by ">" between the notation and TAB staves). These notes, which coincide with the band's bashing of buckets and other goodies in the background, are supposed to be emphasized. To get them to "pop" out at the necessary volume, simply dig in with your pick every time you see a ">."

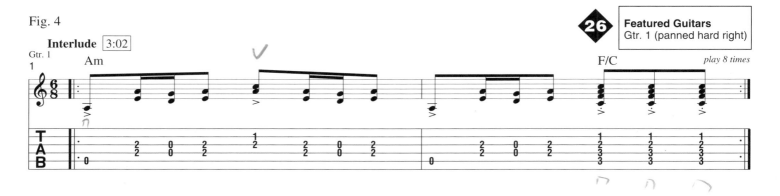

## Figure 5—Outro

This outro figure is the first and only instance in "Breaking the Girl" where an electric guitar (Gtr. 2, w/clean tone) is used. While Gtr. 1 restates the song's chorus figure (Rhy. Fig. 1), Gtr. 2 engages in a melodic figure that gets its flavor from the repetition of several *dyads* (two-note chord partials) located at the twelfth position. These dyads are performed in the same rhythmic manner throughout and doubled similarly with a mellotron played by the album's engineer, Brendan O'Brien.

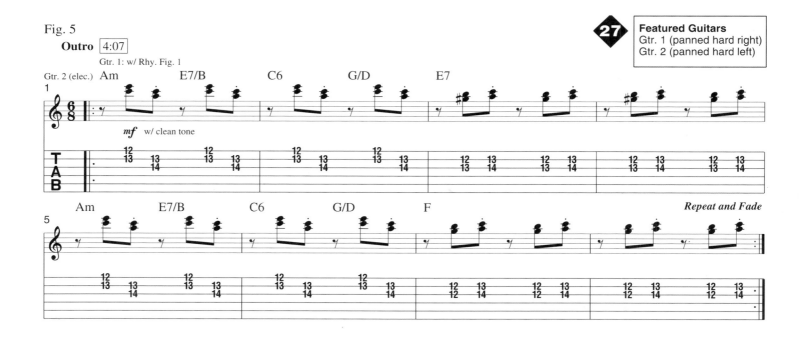

# GIVE IT AWAY

**Words and Music by Anthony Kiedis, Flea, Chad Smith and John Frusciante**

"Give It Away" is a manic display of vintage-style Red Hot Chili Peppers. With Anthony's rapid-fire rapping, the clever combination of Flea's simple bass line with John's syncopated guitar riff, and Chad's ferocious skin pounding, this first single (released in August 1991) from *BloodSugarSexMagik* proved to skeptics across the globe that the success of their previous album, *Mother's Milk,* was far from any funky fluke. Accompanied by a brilliantly shot black-and-white video, "Give It Away" won "Best Breakthrough Video" at the MTV Music Awards in September 1992 and earned the band a "Best Hard Rock Song" award at the Grammys in February 1993.

### Figure 1—Intro

John kicks things off in this tune with some droning A *octave shapes* (between the open A string and the seventh fret of the D string), and some obnoxiously syncopated, disturbing string-bending licks—all on top of Chad's driving funk-rock groove. An "octave" is a musical interval that consists of two or more notes eight scale tones apart. (The prefix *oct-* means "eight.") For more dirt on octaves, flip forward to "Warped," Figure 4.

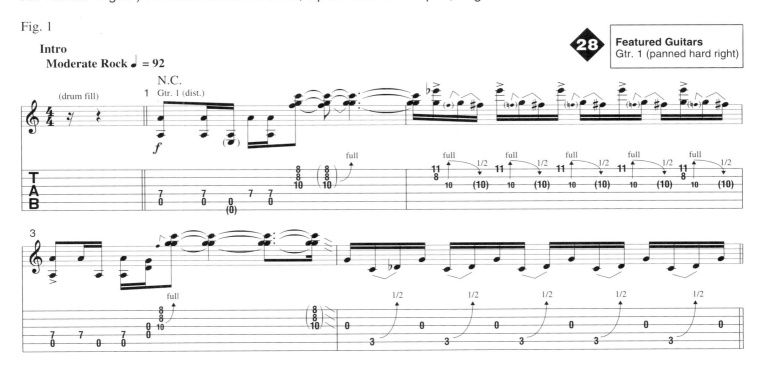

Fig. 1

Intro
Moderate Rock ♩ = 92

Featured Guitars
Gtr. 1 (panned hard right)

### Figure 2—Verse

While Flea bangs out his repetitive bass line, John engages in a brilliantly syncopated, single-note riff that makes clever use of *chromatic passing tones*. This riff is loosely based on the A minor pentatonic scale (A–C–D–E–G) in the fifth position. In many instances, however, John creates tension within this scale by squeezing in extra notes outside of the scale, passing between the notes D and C with the note C♯ in measure 1, and between D and E with the note D♯ in measure 2. These notes (C♯ and D♯) are considered to be "chromatic passing tones" because they are outside of the A minor pentatonic scale and are used to "pass" between the theoretically "correct" notes.

Fig. 2

**Verse** [0:11]

Featured Guitars
Gtr. 1 (panned hard right)

## Figure 3—Chorus

While Anthony barks, "Give it away, give it away, give it away now," John returns to his A octave figure (à la the intro), performing it in steady sixteenth notes throughout this chorus riff. Notice how John spices things up in the latter halves of measures 2 and 4 with some A minor pentatonic, Chuck Berry-style licks.

Fig. 3

**Chorus** [0:42]

Featured Guitars
Gtr. 1 (panned hard right)

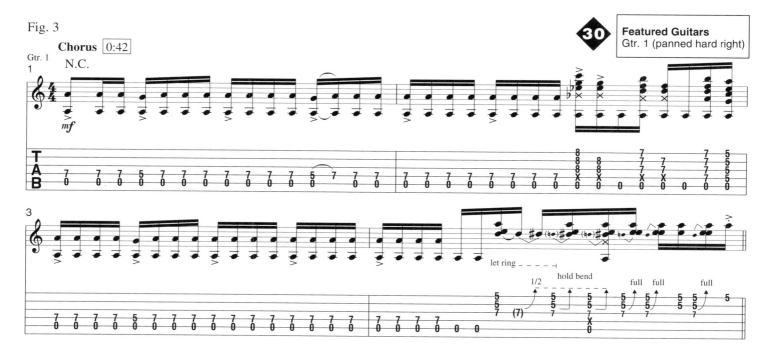

**Figure 4—First Guitar Solo**

Both guitar solos in this tune were recorded backwards, meaning that John actually *flipped over the master tape* after he, Flea, and Chad had recorded the song's basic tracks. The playback of this flipped tape produced the *sound* of the Chili Peppers' Red-Hot rhythm section playing backwards. It was this sound that John then improvised over, recording his normal-sounding leadwork over an abnormal-sounding accompaniment track. When he was done, John flipped the tape over again, returning the rhythm tracks to their original sound, leaving the lead guitar sounding backwards!

In the transcription that follows, John's backwards guitar solo has been arranged for a regular, forward-sounding guitar. To best emulate Frusciante's backwards intentions, try using a volume pedal to swell the envelope of sound after the initial attack of each picked note. This will help you recreate the reversed attack and decay sound of the lead phrases from John's original backwards solo.

While John (Gtr. 2) blazes away, an additional guitar (Gtr. 1) bangs out a repetitive E octave riff. Anthony Kiedis plays this part when the band performs live.

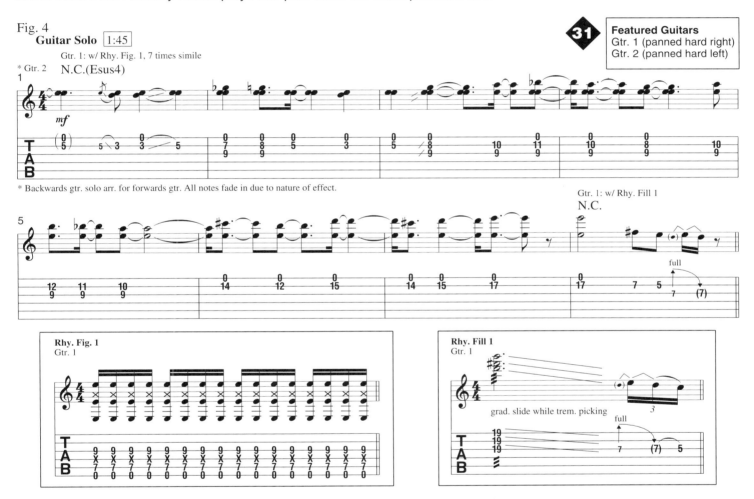

Fig. 4
**Guitar Solo** 1:45

**31** Featured Guitars
Gtr. 1 (panned hard right)
Gtr. 2 (panned hard left)

* Backwards gtr. solo arr. for forwards gtr. All notes fade in due to nature of effect.

**Figure 5—Final Chorus**

For the first four measures of this last chorus, Frusciante brings back the song's intro riff and tacks on some piercing, three-note chordal tidbits at the end (measures 2 and 4). These note groupings are derived primarily from A minor pentatonic (A–C–D–E–G) as John flattens out his index finger across the seventeenth fret to grab the notes A, E, and C across the top three strings. He then gropes even higher on his fretboard, barring across the twentieth fret with his third finger to access the notes C, G, and E♭—the latter note being the only pitch foreign to A minor pentatonic and the primary source of this riff's dissonance.

In measures 5–12, John engages in some chromatic craftsmanship similar to what was encountered in the earlier verse figure, squeezing a chromatic passing tone in between the notes D and C along the third string. Notice how Frusciante shies away from any sort of predictability by varying the rhythms of this phrase, spicing up the line on occasion with some more of his inventive octave work (measures 9–10).

Fig. 5

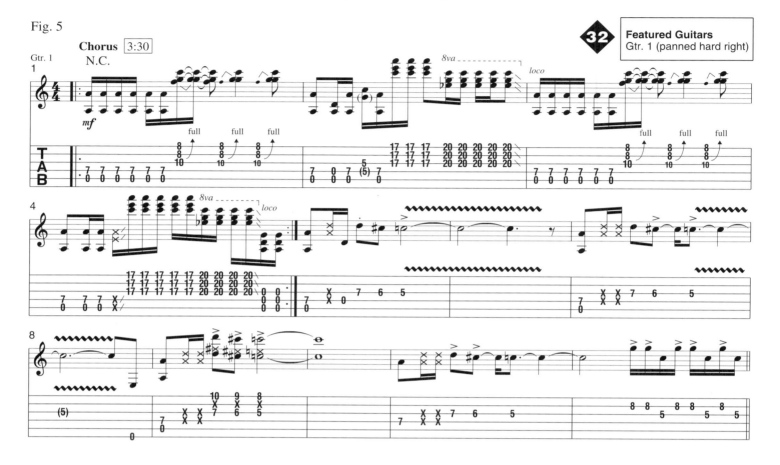

## Figure 6—Outro

The outro to "Give It Away" marks the first time Frusciante plays any traditional chords during this song, rocking out with a series of power chords—A5, D5, Db5, and C5 (Gtr. 3)—in a repeated, one-measure riff. Meanwhile, Gtr. 1 engages in some of the same types of brash pentatonic note groupings (seventeenth position) explored in the previous chorus.

Fig. 6

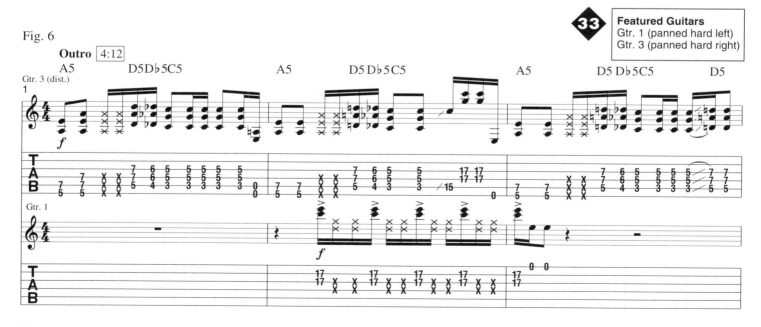

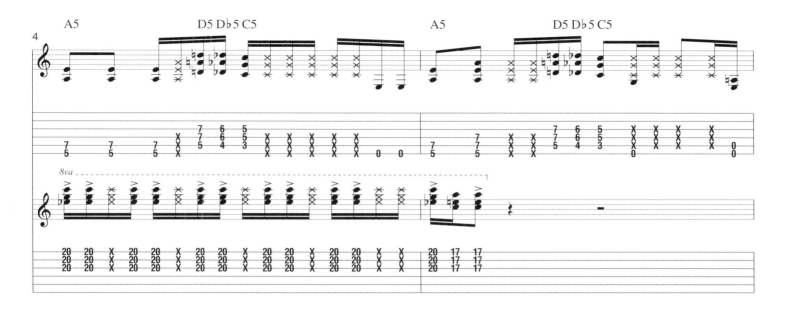

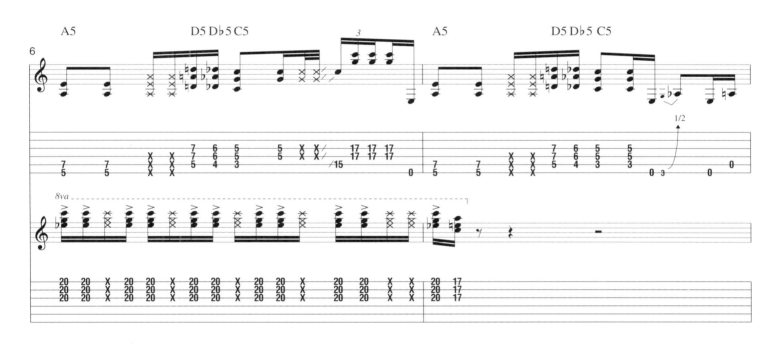

# UNDER THE BRIDGE

**Words and Music by Anthony Kiedis, Flea, Chad Smith and John Frusciante**

"Under the Bridge" was the commercial hit that propelled the Red Hot Chili Peppers into the mainstream spotlight. Though it was released as the second single from *BloodSugarSexMagik* in February of 1992 (it eventually reached #2), this song might not have ever left the confines of Anthony Kiedis's creative mind if it had not been for the words of encouragement from the album's producer, Rick Rubin.

On a day when Kiedis and Rubin were going over sheets of completed lyrics, Rubin came across a page that Anthony had never intended anyone to see. It was an autobiographical piece that illustrated Anthony's painful recollection of a time (Fall '86) when he frequently met with a band of gang members under a particular bridge in downtown Los Angeles with the intentions of scoring heroin. Due to the sensitive nature of the song's subject matter, and the fact that Rubin's past work included recording heavy bands like Public Enemy, the Beastie Boys, and Run DMC, Anthony never even considered showing these lyrics to Rubin. He hadn't even shown them to the band yet. Since the point of the meeting was to go over everything the Red Hot Chili Peppers had, Rubin encouraged Anthony to sing it for him. The song, which was entitled "Under the Bridge," floored Rubin. The band, when it finally heard the song for the first time, reacted the same way.

**Figure 1—Intro**

If you've seen the Red Hot Chili Peppers' video for this song, you've probably seen John Frusciante at the beginning grabbing some pretty unorthodox looking chords. The fact is, these chords are exact transpositions of two open-position chords you probably already know—C and E, moved up one whole step to fully-fretted versions of D and F♯, respectively. John uses fingerstyle technique to play this arpeggiated passage, meaning that he uses the thumb (*p*), index (*i*), middle (*m*), and ring (*a*) fingers of his picking hand (John holds his pick in his mouth during this passage) to articulate the strings.

Fig. 1

**Intro**

**Moderately Slow** ♩ = 68

band tacet

Gtr. 1 (elec.)

## Figure 2—First Verse

Returning the pick to his hand, John creates some great accompanimental textures throughout the verse sections of this song, cramming in a handful of classic Hendrix-inspired rhythm guitar ideas in every measure as a means of sprucing up basic moveable chord shapes. For the first verse, John keeps things relatively simple by modestly strumming a series of stock moveable chord shapes: E, B, C#m, G#m, and A. Notice that he omits the lowest root note (which would normally be found on the sixth string) in the C#m, G#m, and A voicings in measures 2 and 6. Between many of these chord changes, John smacks his muted strings to achieve a percussive effect. This gives his groove a little extra snap since Flea and Chad haven't entered the picture yet. Frusciante's ten-measure chord progression is punctuated with an Emaj7 chord in measure 9, marking Flea and Chad's initial entrance.

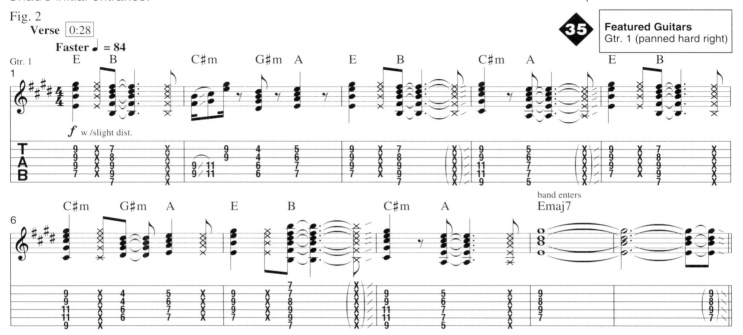

## Figure 3—Second and Third Verses

John pays homage to one of his heroes, Jimi Hendrix, throughout the second and third verses with a smattering of clever embellishments to the basic chord shapes introduced in the first verse. Using everything from two-note chord partials, hammer-ons/pull-offs, double stops, and arpeggiation techniques, Frusciante succeeds in inventing a timeless chordal figure of his own without sounding like a Hendrix ripoff.

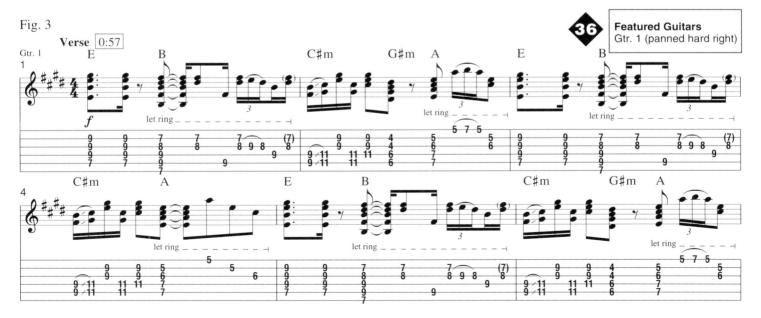

43

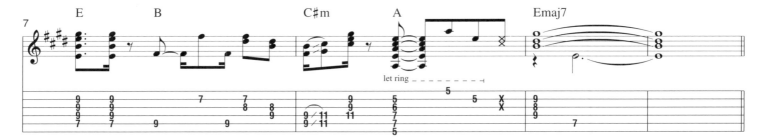

## Figure 4—Pre-Chorus

Alternating between the chords F♯m, E, and B in this pre-chorus passage, John once again opts to funk things up a bit by smacking a handful of muted strings between chords (measures 2–4). Notice that each of the three chords in this section have their lower root notes positioned along the fifth string, exclusively. This provides you with the challenge of switching between two different moveable chord shapes (major and minor) as they occur along the fretboard, since the notes that form each chord are consistently confined to the same string set (strings 2–5).

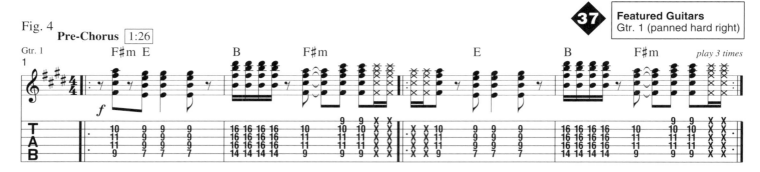

## Figure 5—Outro

This outro figure is based on the same chord progression performed in the chorus section but is much more elaborate and easier to hear because the massive wall of background vocals cease at this point. John explores unisons and dissonances in this strummed passage, amidst more hammer-ons/pull-offs and arpeggiated chord fragments in the tradition of the second and third verses.

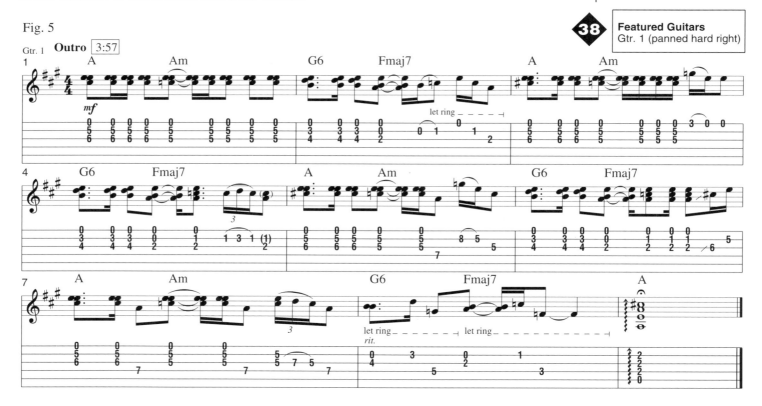

# One Hot Minute

For reasons undisclosed, as of June 1993, Arik Marshall was officially out of the Red Hot Chili Peppers. A massive "cattle-call" audition process ensued where over 3000 guitarists were given the opportunity to see if they had what it took to become a Pepper. None of them were chosen. Anthony heard a guy named Jesse Tobias jamming at a club and asked him to join. Tobias was in the band for about two weeks before being replaced by Dave Navarro. (Tobias would later end up as a member of Alanis Morissette's touring band on a referral from Flea.)

After hooking up with Navarro, the Red Hot Chili Peppers rehearsed for a bit, then flew to Hawaii where the newly-formed quartet of funksters bonded and wrote most of the tunes for their forthcoming album, *One Hot Minute*. With Rick Rubin producing, the album was recorded in a handful of studios throughout the Los Angeles area (Grand Master, Ocean Way, Sound City, and Hollywood Sound studios). The end result was a classic combination of Anthony Kiedis's pristine poetry, Flea's bombastic bass work, Chad Smith's raging rock rhythms, and the chunky-yet-funky, ethereal guitar stylings of Chilean newcomer, Dave Navarro.

From the get-go, Dave's atmospheric influence on the band's ever-evolving compositional style became immediately apparent. Songs like "Warped," "Aeroplane," and "My Friends" demonstrated Navarro's knack for creating everything from psychedelic song textures (courtesy of multiple delay-drenched, wah-pedal-tinged overdubs) and in-your-face metal grooves (in the spirit of vintage Led Zeppelin) to Hendrix-inspired guitar madness and atonal riffage—an approach that vastly differed from Dave's funky forefathers (Slovak and Frusciante), who favored a more traditional, stripped-down approach towards composition and recording.

# WARPED

**Words and Music by Anthony Kiedis, Flea,
Chad Smith and David Navarro**

"Warped," the opening cut off of *One Hot Minute*, was the first single and video released from the album and clearly demonstrates the band's increased diversity with the addition of guitarist Dave Navarro.

Dave used Fender Custom Shop Stratocasters for most of the songs on *One Hot Minute*. He had been playing Paul Reed Smith guitars since his days in Jane's Addiction, but switched to Stratocasters in order to accommodate the Chili Peppers' older material when playing live. Dave liked the instrument so much that he stuck with it. He also used Marshall JCM 900s, Bogner Ecstasy heads, and an old Silvertone amp on the album.

### Figure 1—Preamble

The opening of this song pits Anthony, Flea, Chad, and Dave in a psychedelic preamble that is performed free of any rhythmic time constraints. Here, Dave's two guitars float loftily over Flea's droning bass line, while Anthony's vocal is treated with heavy delay effects, further contributing to this section's ethereal soundscape with the utterance of "My tendency for dependency is offending me."

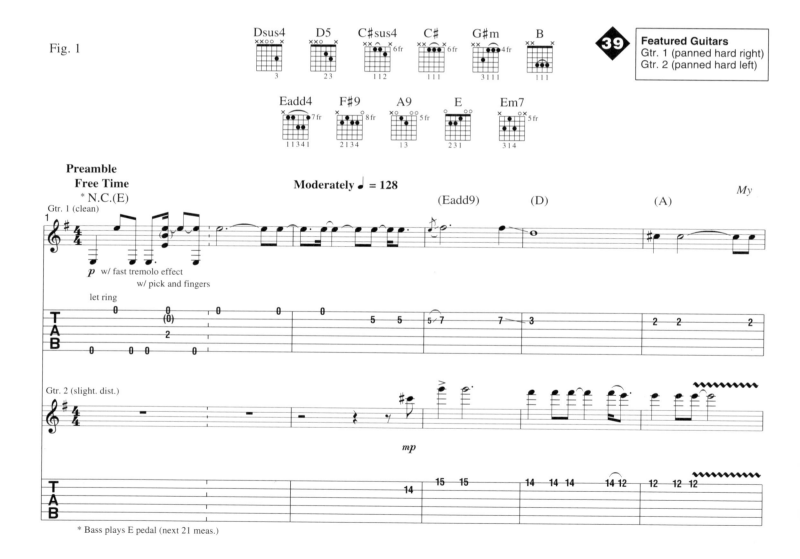

Fig. 1

**Featured Guitars**
Gtr. 1 (panned hard right)
Gtr. 2 (panned hard left)

* Bass plays E pedal (next 21 meas.)

*ten-den-cy. for de-pen-den - cy is of-fend-ing me...*

\* w/ vol. knob

## Figure 2—Intro

When listeners least expect it, the Red Hot Chili Peppers' rhythm section launches into a driving rock groove in the tradition of some of the heaviest Led Zeppelin, amidst Anthony's bellowing grunts. This four-measure section is comprised of a repeated one-measure, single-note riff (Riff A), which Dave and Flea play in unison. The figure is restated throughout each of the verse sections, portions of the chorus, and is also used to punctuate Dave Navarro's guitar solo.

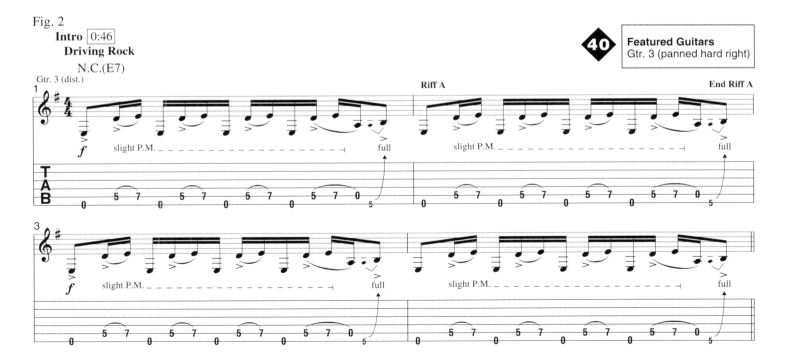

Fig. 2
**Intro** 0:46
**Driving Rock**

## Figure 3—First Chorus

The first half of this chorus figure involves the repetition of a one-measure chord riff that alternates between Dsus4 and D5 (Rhy. Fig. 1), presented here in slash notation. Notice that these chords are performed in the same rhythmic manner that Anthony chooses to sing the vocal, "all the way, all the way," in measures 3–4. Immediately following this lyric statement, Flea and Dave resume the single-note riff that propelled the earlier intro and verse sections (Riff A).

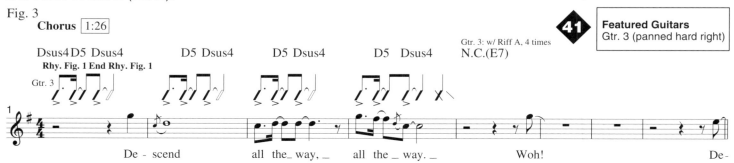

## Figure 4—Second Chorus

After four measures of Rhy. Fig. 1, Gtr. 4 makes its first appearance with the performance of some of Dave's trademark octave shapes. Used in conjunction with an echo device, this type of sonority fattens up the sound of Dave's improvised melodies—a necessity when the band performs live, since Dave's guitar functions as the only harmonic instrument in the group. Notice here that Dave confines his octave shapes to the third and fifth strings exclusively, sliding in and out of notes from D Mixolydian (D–E–F#–G–A–B–C) over the Dsus4 and D5 chords performed by Gtr. 3.

To cleanly execute these sliding octave shapes, you're going to need to rely heavily on fret-hand muting. This technique is necessary because you will be playing two notes simultaneously on a pair of strings that are not adjacent to one another; you will need to silence the fourth string so that no unintentional pitches are produced on it. To accomplish this, fret the lower note of each octave (fifth string) with your first finger and the higher note (third string) with your third finger, then arch part of your first finger over the fourth string so that it lightly comes into contact with it, without actually fretting a note. This will prevent any sound from being produced when you strike the fourth string with your pick. Fret-hand muting is an invaluable technique in all aspects of guitar playing and, when under control, will help polish up your fret-hand chops in general.

## Figure 5—Guitar Solo

At the beginning of this solo, Dave kicks in a delay device that he's set to echo back his introductory lead statements in a fading eighth-note pulse (352 milliseconds at this tempo)—all over the tonality of A5 (implied by Gtr. 3). His creative use of delay effects maximizes the dramatic impact of his sparse playing at this point in the solo, since he chooses to play primarily just one note on the first beat of measures 1, 3, 5, and 7. In this solo's latter measures (9–16), check out how effectively Dave sculpts his melodic statements, despite the fact that he's playing steady sixteenth notes. Derived primarily from A Dorian (A–B–C–D–E–F♯–G), the contour of the line he structures while relentlessly picking in steady sixteenths has powerful melodic impact in and of itself, without having to rely on any sort of rhythmic inventiveness to keep things interesting. Dave winds down this sixteenth-note barrage by introducing the note C♯—the major third in the key of A—in measure 15, superimposing a major tonality over a minor key.

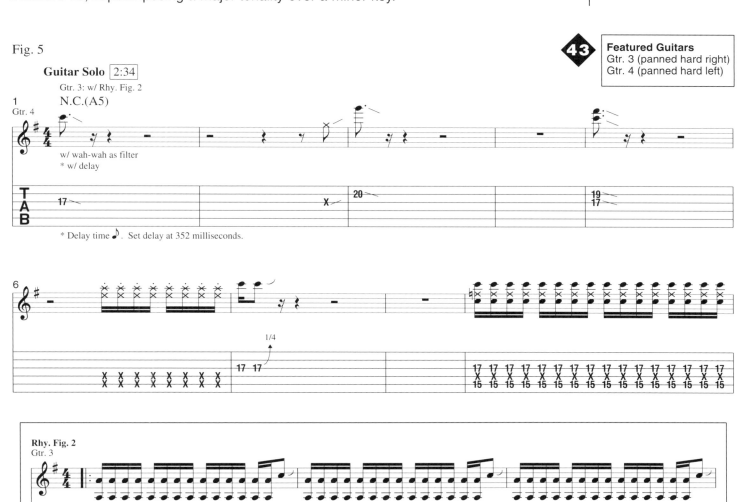

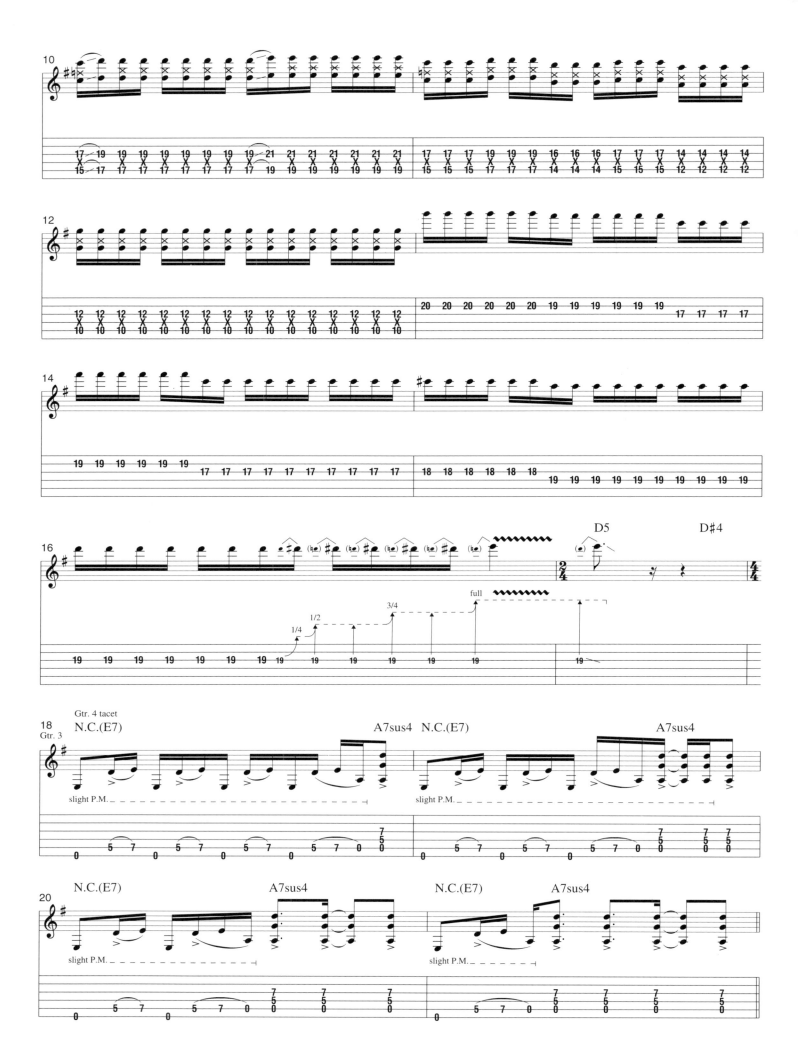

## Figure 6—Outro

You really get your money's worth with this Chili Peppers tune! In this outro section, the band provides us with yet another shift in their musical gears—a change in tempo (slower), dynamics (quieter), and overall vibe (mellower). Dave pilots the ship from here on out with his textural playing, arpeggiating a lush arrangement of chords (C#sus4, C#, G#m, B, G#m, etc.) on one guitar (Gtr. 4), while strumming the same chord shapes on another (Gtr. 3, in slashes). As this tune winds down, the band segues into another one of their hits from *One Hot Minute*, "Aeroplane."

# AEROPLANE

**Words and Music by Anthony Kiedis, Flea,
Chad Smith and David Navarro**

"Aeroplane" was one of the first songs completed prior to the recording of *One Hot Minute*. The Red Hot Chili Peppers even performed it during their Woodstock '94 and European tour sets prior to the album's release. Flea's daughter, Clara, makes a special guest appearance on the album version as a member of the "kid choir" that is heard during some of the song's chorus sections.

### Figure 1—Intro

Throughout this song's intro, Dave Navarro lays down a bed of lush, arpeggiated chords, while Flea provides a handful of melodic fills in the background. Dave ran his guitar direct into the recording console to achieve the squeaky clean Stratocaster tones that dominate the majority of "Aeroplane." In measure 7 of this intro figure, an additional guitar (Gtr. 2) enters the picture with a two-note chord (see Fill 1). While this pair of notes is sustained, Dave gradually depresses his whammy bar to the point where the notes gurgle, the slackened strings flopping against his guitar's pickups (beat 4 in the last measure of Fill 1).

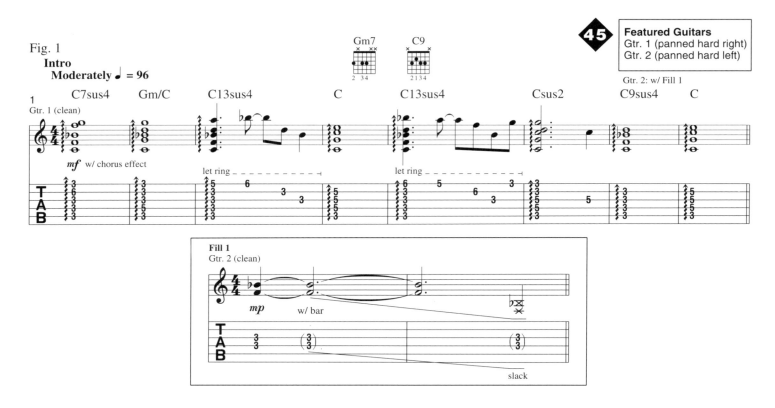

### Figure 2—Chorus

The initial statement of this song's chorus is heard immediately following Dave and Flea's eight-measure intro and involves a steady sixteenth-note strumming pattern, alternating between two chords positioned along the top three strings—Gm11 and C7 (Rhy. Fig. 1). So that your strums are as rhythmically precise as possible, confine the motion of your pick hand to your wrist (keep it relaxed), and rotate from it using consistent down-up strokes. This should help you lock into Dave's groove as your pick slices almost mechanically through the top three strings.

Dave varies the texture of this chorus section in measure 5 with some single-note fills from a wah-soaked guitar (Gtr. 2). This style of syncopated sixteenth-note riffing is one of the hippest and most effective ways of funking up a section of a tune that is based on a repeated chord cycle. Dave rocks back and forth on his wah-wah pedal as he improvises this four-measure line, using notes from G minor pentatonic (G–B♭–C–D–F) in and around the third position.

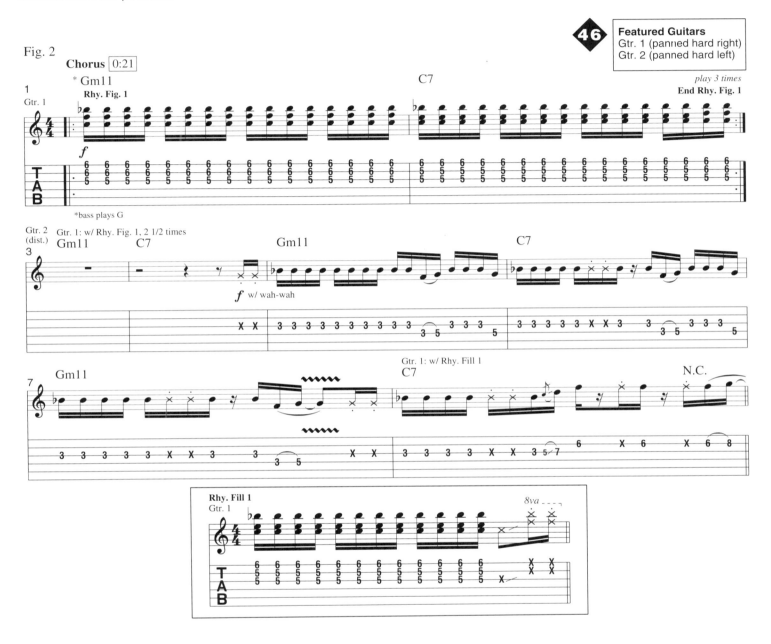

## Figure 3—Second Verse

Throughout this verse section, one of Dave's guitars (Gtr. 1) manages to imply the same Gm7-to-C7 progression introduced in the chorus using only two-note chords. These dyads consist of the third and seventh chord tones from Gm7 and C7 (Gm7: ♭3=B♭, ♭7=F; C7: 3=E, ♭7= B♭) and are a minimalist means of suggesting the same progression without performing the exact same figure.

While Gtr. 1 smacks its two-note chords (Rhy. Fig. 2), Gtr. 3 makes the scene in measure 4, enriching the soundscape with some more syncopated sixteenth notes—this time performed much more sporadically, with a clean tone and a phase shifter. The overall vibe that Dave achieves with this unpredictable line is reminiscent of some of Bootsy Collins's brilliant, phase-shifted, melodic bass work on several of the funkiest Parliament/Funkadelic tracks.

Fig. 3

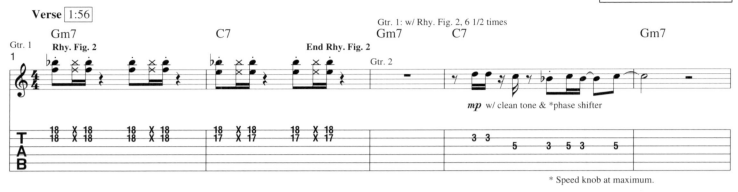

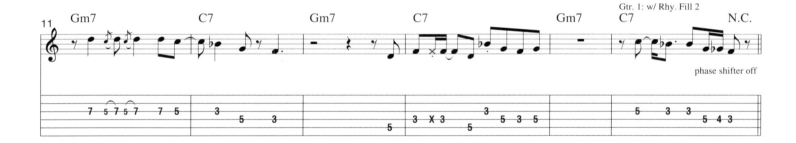

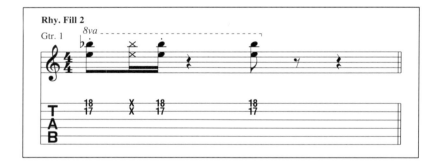

## Figure 4—Bridge

Dave returns to more steady sixteenth-note strumming in this bridge figure, pulling listeners into a new harmonic direction as new chords are introduced (B♭5/E♭, B♭/F, F6, Gm, etc.). At this point, the entire band backs off a bit in volume, achieving a different mood by their subtle shift in dynamics. As you've probably noticed by now, Dave is a big fan of using multiple guitars to achieve textural variety within a song. In measure 5, Gtr. 2 enters the mix once again, floating over the repetition of Rhy. Fig. 3. This second guitar sustains each of its chords throughout this section, as opposed to engaging in the type of strumming performed by Gtr. 1. Dave also adds some of his trademark wah-wah pedal inflections to these resonating chords, making them cry as he rapidly oscillates his foot forward and back.

Fig. 4

## Figure 5—Outro-Guitar Solo

Immediately after a masterful bass demonstration (courtesy of the flamboyant Flea-ster), Dave launches into the outro-guitar solo depicted below. Here, Dave proceeds to rock out with a smattering of licks derived from G minor pentatonic (G–Bb–C–D–F) in various positions (fifteenth position in measures 1–8; fluctuating between the third and sixth positions in measures 9–17), with the occasional addition of the notes A (seventeenth fret, first string) and E (fifth fret, second string). These notes Dave throws in (A in measure 2, E in measures 15–16) are not mere passing tones between pentatonic pitches, but rather allude to the completed G Dorian scale (G–A–Bb–C–D–E–F–G). After *tremolo picking* (picking all notes as rapidly as possible) a three-note version of a G7 chord in measures 18–19 while the rest of the band floats in "free time," this song's final moments act as a segue into the album's next track, "Deep Kick."

Fig. 5

**Featured Guitars**
Gtr. 1 (panned hard left)
Gtr. 2 (panned hard right)

* Gtrs. play w/ triplet feel, next 16 meas.

56

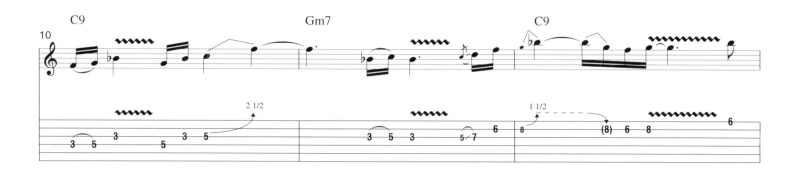

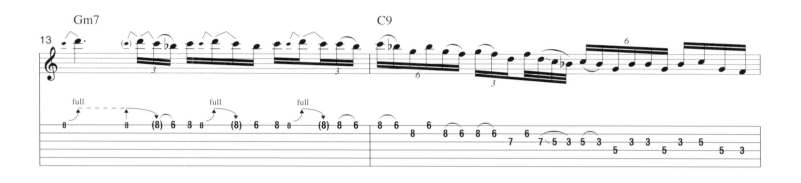

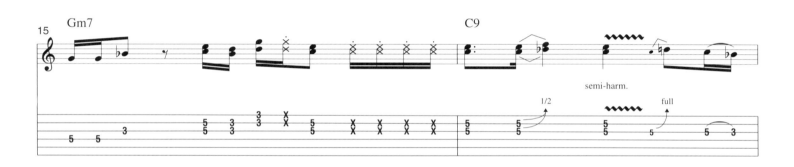

**Free Time**

*Segue to "Deep Kick"*

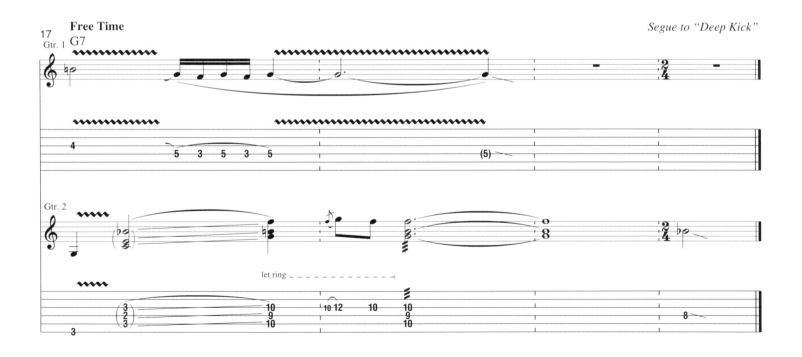

# MY FRIENDS

**Words and Music by Anthony Kiedis, Flea, Chad Smith and David Navarro**

The second single from *One Hot Minute*, "My Friends" demonstrates Dave's adeptness in manipulating acoustic and electric guitar textures to create a soundscape that masterfully complements Anthony's melodic vocal. Flea actually composed most of this song on his acoustic guitar, then Dave came in and created his own parts, embellishing the track with his trademark studio overdubbing. For some insights into Dave's creative approach in the studio and his multitracking madness, check out what he revealed in an interview with *Guitar World* magazine:

> *"I don't set out to record zillions of tracks. I always start out thinking I'll go really minimal, but I never seem to like one of my own tracks by itself, though I like it when other players use just a single track. I might double the rhythms and think, 'Wow, that sounds better.' And no matter how good the rhythms sound, I never like to leave just rhythm guitar, especially not big power chords. I like to be more multi-dimensional. Anyway, the more the song gets played, the more little holes I hear where something could fit, and all that time I have the echoes and ambience in my head, even if they're not on the track yet. I guess I'd rather have too many guitars on tape and pull tracks away when we mix, as opposed to sitting there during the mix saying, 'Wow, I wish I'd done that or doubled this.' "*

### Figure 1—Intro/First Verse

Make sure that you've tuned the sixth string of your acoustic guitar down one whole step to D (one octave lower than the open fourth string) before diving into this tune. Track 4 on the accompanying CD should help you tune your instrument to the appropriate pitches. Throughout "My Friends," Drop D tuning allows guitarist Dave Navarro to expand upon the sonic range of Gtr. 2 and access chords and textures that couldn't be achieved by way of standard tuning.

The four-measure intro figure to "My Friends" features two acoustic guitars (Gtr. 1 in standard tuning) and is restated similarly as the primary accompaniment for each verse. The riff itself involves the arpeggiation of the open-position chords Dsus2, Dm(add9)/F, G/B, and C(add9)—some colorful variations on the fairly common "cowboy chords" D, Dm, G, and C. Notice how Dave takes advantage of the tuning of Gtr. 2 in measures 4–5 and 8–9, using its dropped-D string as a thickening agent to fatten up the song's mix and reinforce the harmony.

Fig. 1

**Featured Guitars**
Gtr. 1 (panned hard left)
Gtr. 2 (panned hard right)

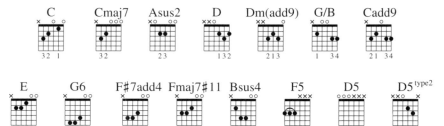

Gtr. 2: Drop D Tuning:
(1) = E (4) = D
(2) = B (5) = A
(3) = G (6) = D

**Intro**

**Moderately Slow ♩ = 84**

* Chord symbols reflect overall tonality.
** bass plays F

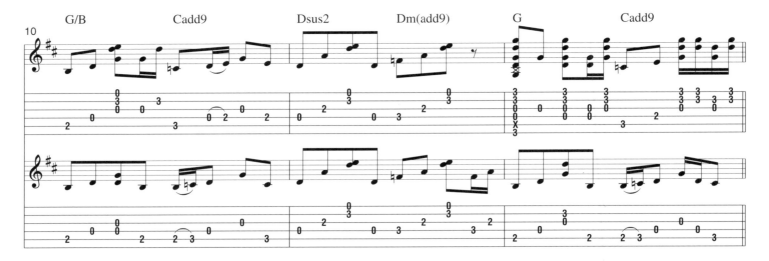

## Figure 2—Second and Third Verses

During the second and third verses, Dave brings a clean-tone electric guitar (Gtr. 3) into the mix, arpeggiating a series of three-note chords voiced on the instrument's top three strings. Aside from contributing more density to the song's texture, this new part makes use of chord tones that differ from those inherent to the acoustic guitar riff studied in the previous figure.

While Gtrs. 1 and 2 perform the chords Dsus2, Dm(add9)/F, G/B, and Cadd9, Gtr. 3 superimposes note groupings that imply the chords D, Dsus4, G7sus4, and C. If you relate each of these chords to each other as they occur simultaneously in the music (e.g., Dsus2 vs. D, Dm (add9)/F vs. Dsus4, etc.), the additional chord tones generated by Gtr. 3 become immediately apparent.

**51** **Featured Guitars**
Gtrs. 1&2 (panned hard right)
Gtr. 3 (panned hard left)

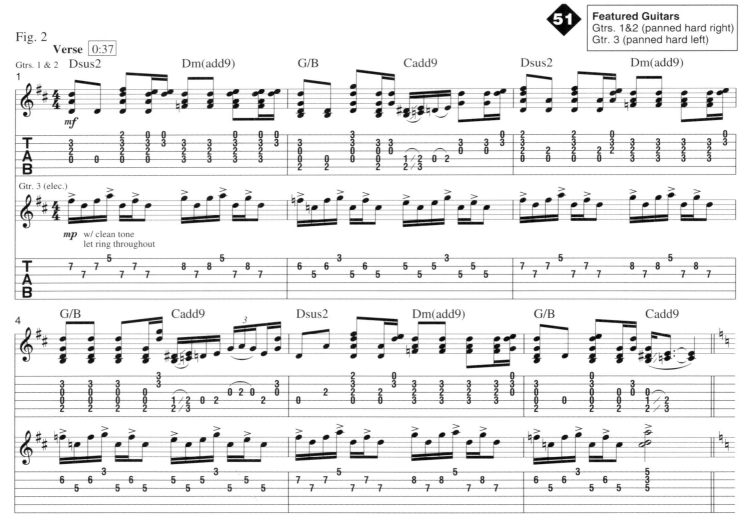

## Figure 3—Chorus

Here's an excerpt from this song's chorus riff that involves a combination of long, sustained chords and arpeggiation techniques. At this point in the song, we encounter a key change to A minor with the performance of the chords C, Asus2, and D in measures 1–3. In measure 4 an Aadd9 chord is introduced, temporarily alluding to the key of A major—the *parallel major* of A minor. Any major or minor keys sharing the same root note (e.g., A minor and A major) are regarded as parallel keys to one another. Within the context of a song, this can be a useful compositional device, as it provides a seemingly instantaneous change of mood from "sad" (minor) to "happy" (major), while maintaining the same root note—A, in this case.

**Featured Guitars**
Gtr. 1 (panned hard left)
Gtr. 2 (panned hard right)
Gtr. 3 (center of mix)

## Figure 4—Guitar Solo

During this guitar solo, Dave slides in and out of D Mixolydian (D–E–F♯–G–A–B–C) using some of his trademark octave shapes. This interval shape surfaces frequently in Dave's improvisatory efforts and also factors into the construction of many of his monstrous guitar riffs. (See "Warped," Figure 4, for more on playing octaves.)

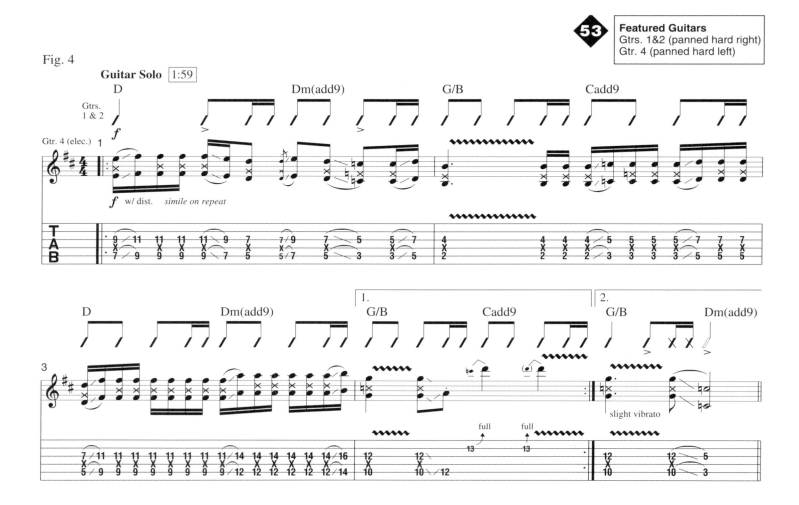

**Featured Guitars**
Gtrs. 1&2 (panned hard right)
Gtr. 4 (panned hard left)

## Figure 5—Bridge

Immediately following Dave's guitar solo, a bridge section ensues that is based upon a pretty radical chord progression—much more harmonically active than in previous sections. At this point, Gtrs. 1 and 2 (written in slashes) churn out the chords E, G6, F♯7add4, Fmaj7♯11, C, Bsus4, and F5, while Gtr. 4 performs some of the same type of octave shapes encountered in the previous guitar solo.

Throughout this bridge riff (Gtrs. 1 and 2) Dave exploits the effectiveness of common tones amidst an assortment of strummed chords. As your fingers grope for these chords (see the chord frames in Figure 1), notice how most of them have the open first (E) and second (B) strings woven into their harmonic fabric. These two open strings act as "common tones" to the chords E, G6, F♯7add4, Fmaj7♯11, and Bsus4 and drastically affect each chord's harmonic color since they remain as a constant pitch, while other fretted notes are moved around with each new chord. In music theory terms, this type of note movement, where one or more notes remain stationary while others move, is called *oblique motion.*

**Featured Guitars**
Gtrs. 1&2 (panned hard right)
Gtr. 4 (panned hard left)

Fig. 5

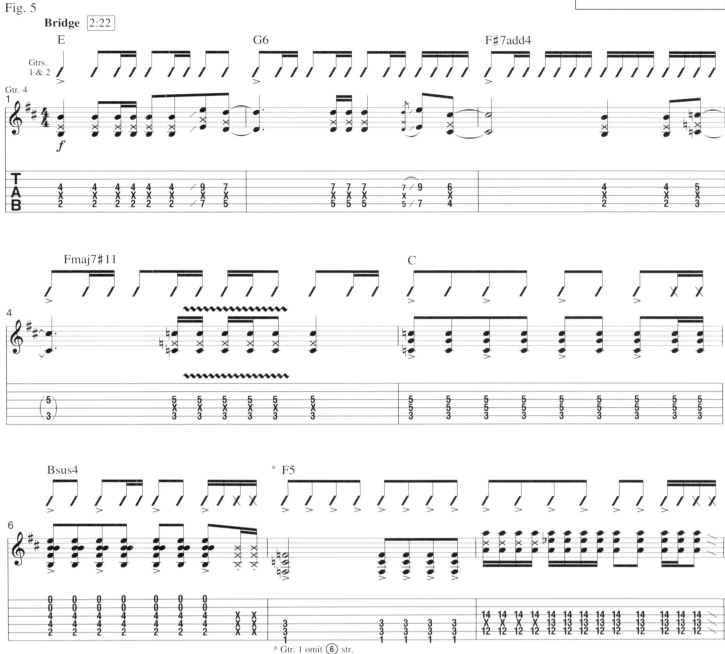

* Gtr. 1 omit ⑥ str.

## Figure 6—Outro

In this outro section, Dave exploits the effectiveness of dissonance in the context of a guitar solo—most notably in the second half of measures 1 and 3 (Gtr. 4). "Dissonance" occurs when two or more notes a certain distance (or interval) apart are allowed to ring together and create a restless or unpleasant sound, which needs to be resolved. The closer these two notes are to each other, the harsher or more dissonant the sound. In the case of measures 1 and 3, dissonance occurs between the notes G (twelfth fret, third string) and A (tenth fret, second string). These two notes form the interval of a major second (two notes that are one whole step apart) and create an unsettling effect when they sound together—especially when they are repeatedly articulated in steady sixteenth notes over a Dm(add9) chord. As was characteristic of the two previous tunes studied from *One Hot Minute*, the conclusion of this song segues into another song, "Coffee Shop."

**Featured Guitars**
Gtr. 1 (panned hard left)
Gtr. 2 (panned hard right)
Gtr. 4 (center of mix)

Fig. 6

**Outro** 3:26

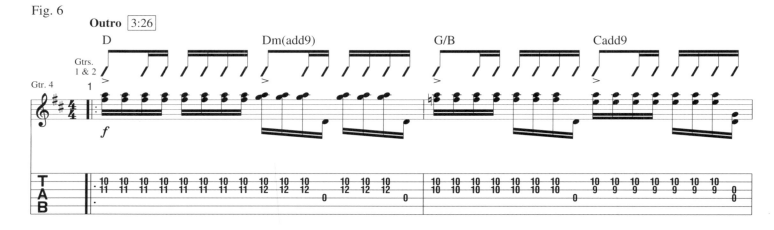

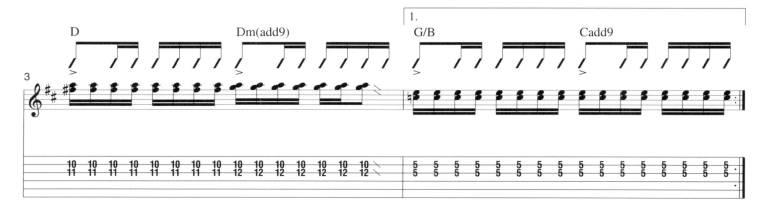

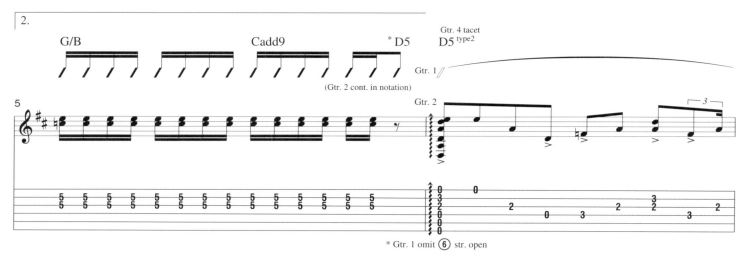

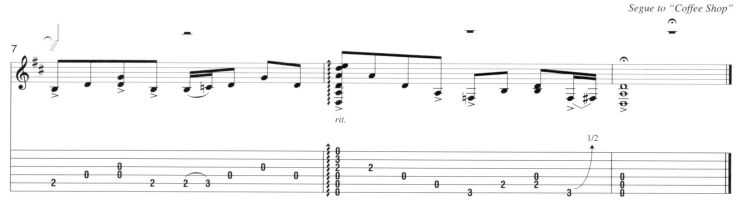

64

# Soundtracks

Over the last few years, entertainment-oriented publications have drawn attention to rockers who have been bitten by the acting bug—Madonna, Glenn Frey, Courtney Love, Jon Bon Jovi... The list could go on and on. But they never seem to credit Anthony or Flea. Believe it or not, this pair has been in more flicks (both as actors and on film soundtracks) than any of the aforementioned rockers-gone-Hollywood. Anthony first appeared in film footage as far back as 1976 with his performance as Cole Dammett—the son of a character played by Sylvester Stallone in the movie *F.I.S.T.* He also played a fairly prominent role alongside Keanu Reeves and Patrick Swayze in *Point Break* (1990). Meanwhile, Flea has been in everything from *Suburbia* and *Back to the Future, Part II* to *Blue Iguana* and *Stranded*. Both Anthony and Flea were actually featured together as a pair of road-trippin' goofballs in another movie, *The Chase*, which starred Charlie Sheen!

Everybody who has followed the career of the Chili Peppers knows, however, that music is the band's main thing. Anthony and Flea's film appearances were just for kicks. A large selection of the Red Hot Chili Peppers' catalog—including some funky covers—have appeared in scores of soundtracks ranging from *Say Anything* ("Taste the Pain"), *Pretty Woman* ("Show Me You Would"), and *Takin' Care of Business* (cover of Bachman Turner Overdrive's "Takin' Care of Business") to *Wayne's World* ("Sikamikanico") and *Howard Stern: Private Parts* ("I Make My Own Rules," with LL Cool J on vocals). The band's 1996 cover of an Ohio Players' tune, "Love Rollercoaster," was the highlight of the *Beavis and Butt-Head Do America* soundtrack and showcased the Chili Peppers' flair for supercharging funky classics.

# LOVE ROLLERCOASTER

**Words and Music by Ralph Middlebrooks, James Williams, Marshall Jones, Leroy Bonner, Clarence Satchell, Willie Beck and Marvin R. Pierce**

"Love Rollercoaster" was originally recorded back in 1975 by the Ohio Players— a tremendously successful funk-influenced band from the seventies—and appeared on their album *Honey*. This classic recording was a critical milestone for the band as it contained a number of popular hits, including "Sweet Sticky Thing," "Fopp," and, of course, "Love Rollercoaster," the latter of which reached #1 on both the pop and R&B charts.

More than twenty years later, the Red Hot Chili Peppers have exposed this timeless tune to a completely new generation via the *Beavis and Butt-Head Do America* soundtrack. Who else would you rather have responsible for resurrecting such a time-honored funk masterpiece?

### Figure 1—Chorus

The primary riff heard throughout "Love Rollercoaster" is a repeated two-measure figure involving three different major chords: C, B♭, and A. Each of these chords is voiced on the top four strings and uses the exact same moveable fingering, just transposed up or down the neck. Dave plays these chords with a clean tone and smacks 'em hard, using the strumming pattern indicated above the notation staff. A few pages back (see "Breaking the Girl"), we focused on counting out rhythms as a means of locking into a steady groove, synchronizing your picking hand to the counting pattern. If you find nailing this strumming figure to be a bit elusive, try approaching this figure the same way.

Once you get a handle on Dave's syncopated strumming pattern, you'll want to further sculpt the sound of these chords by copping his wrist-snapping *staccato* articulations. "Staccato" (indicated by the placement of a dot "." above or below the affected note) directs a performer to play a note (or chord, in this case) quickly, separating it from the notes before and after it. This can be accomplished by simply releasing the pressure of your fret-hand fingers from each of the notes of the chord, preventing them from ringing out for their full duration.

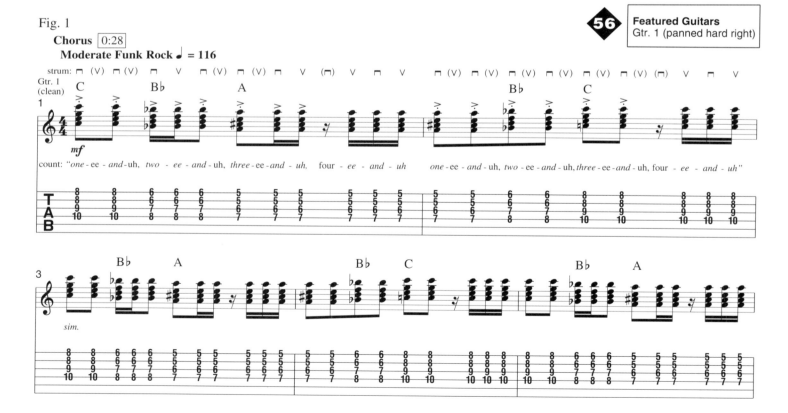

Fig. 1

**56** Featured Guitars
Gtr. 1 (panned hard right)

**Chorus** [0:28]
**Moderate Funk Rock** ♩ = 116

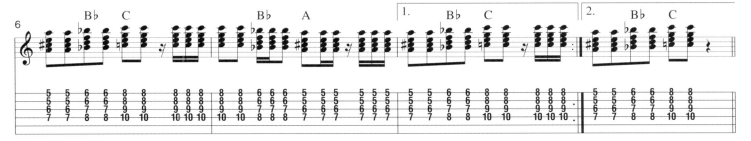

## Figure 2—First Bridge

After kicking in some distortion to supercharge this bridge riff, Dave exploits the jangly effects of open-string power chords. Notice how he frets a huge percentage of the chords in this section in a manner that allows the open third string to sound (measures 1, 3, 5, 7–8). As Dave moves the fretted notes of his atypical power chord shape (measure 1, beat 2) from Fsus2 to G5 (beat 3), the constant reiteration of the open third string acts as a thread running throughout this section, hammering home its G minor tonality.

In instances where Dave plays chords that don't involve open strings, he often opts to intensify the musical moment by applying some wicked vibrato—courtesy of his tremolo bar—to his fretted notes (measures 2 and 4, beat 1). He also makes these chords pulsate by tweaking their pitch a bit with a couple of rapid tremolo bar dips (measure 2, beat 3). A "tremolo bar dip" is created whenever the bar is quickly depressed and released, forcing the note (or chord, in this case) to waver in and out of tune. This is indicated above the notation and TAB staves with a directional pointer and a specification of the interval distance ("-1/2" means lower the pitch by 1/2 step). In the song's outro section, Dave dabbles in even more whammy-bar wackiness.

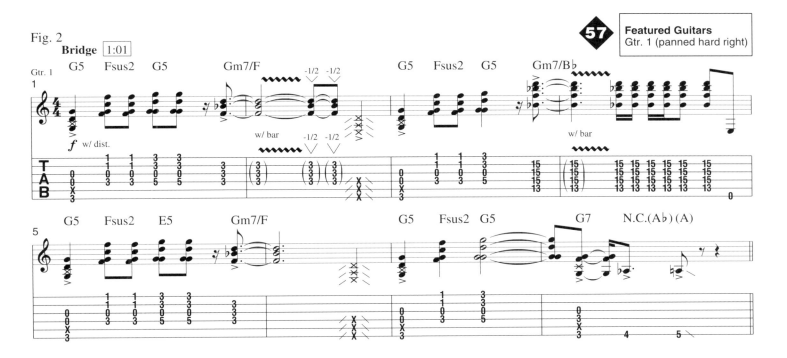

## Figure 3—Outro

Dave cuts loose in this outro section, spewing forth a handful of open-position G minor pentatonic lines (G–Bb–C–D–F) in measures 1–7, with the occasional addition of the note Db—a *chromatic "b5" passing tone* (the "blue" or "lowered" fifth, often used in blues music to create musical tension). The note E also pops up in measure 4, implying the completed G Dorian scale (G–A–Bb–C–D–E–F). Notice that Dave and Flea play in unison throughout the majority of this eight-measure figure.

Dave makes effective use of classic phrasing devices like string bending, hammer-ons/pull-offs, and pinch harmonics throughout this lengthy passage—including some gnarly vibrato-bar pitch bends/dives. On the original recording, Dave's manic guitar activities are a bit obscured by the thunderous vocal track. This book's accompanying audio package will give you an opportunity to clearly hear the types of licks Dave laid down, boosted in volume and performed minus the massive wall of vocals.

Fig. 3

**Outro** 3:39

# GUITAR NOTATION LEGEND

Guitar Music can be notated three different ways: on a *musical staff*, in *tablature*, and in *rhythm slashes*.

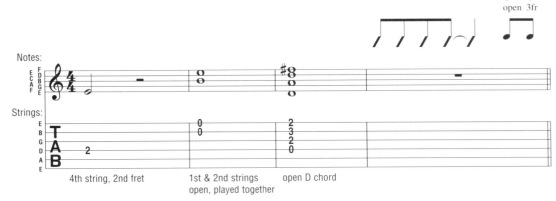

**RHYTHM SLASHES** are written above the staff. Strum chords in the rhythm indicated. Use the chord diagrams found at the top of the first page of the transcription for the appropriate chord voicings. Round noteheads indicate single notes.

**THE MUSICAL STAFF** shows pitches and rhythms and is divided by bar lines into measures. Pitches are named after the first seven letters of the alphabet.

**TABLATURE** graphically represents the guitar fingerboard. Each horizontal line represents a a string, and each number represents a fret.

4th string, 2nd fret

1st & 2nd strings open, played together

open D chord

# DEFINITIONS FOR SPECIAL GUITAR NOTATION

**HALF-STEP BEND:** Strike the note and bend up 1/2 step.

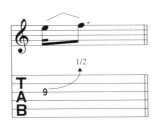

**WHOLE-STEP BEND:** Strike the note and bend up one step.

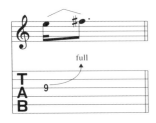

**GRACE NOTE BEND:** Strike the note and bend up as indicated. The first note does not take up any time.

**SLIGHT (MICROTONE) BEND:** Strike the note and bend up 1/4 step.

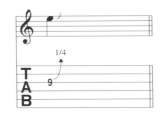

**BEND AND RELEASE:** Strike the note and bend up as indicated, then release back to the original note. Only the first note is struck.

**PRE-BEND:** Bend the note as indicated, then strike it.

**PRE-BEND AND RELEASE:** Bend the note as indicated. Strike it and release the bend back to the original note.

**UNISON BEND:** Strike the two notes simultaneously and bend the lower note up to the pitch of the higher.

**VIBRATO:** The string is vibrated by rapidly bending and releasing the note with the fretting hand.

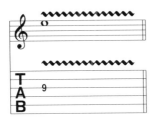

**WIDE VIBRATO:** The pitch is varied to a greater degree by vibrating with the fretting hand.

**HAMMER-ON:** Strike the first (lower) note with one finger, then sound the higher note (on the same string) with another finger by fretting it without picking.

**PULL-OFF:** Place both fingers on the notes to be sounded. Strike the first note and without picking, pull the finger off to sound the second (lower) note.

**LEGATO SLIDE:** Strike the first note and then slide the same fret-hand finger up or down to the second note. The second note is not struck.

**SHIFT SLIDE:** Same as legato slide, except the second note is struck.

**TRILL:** Very rapidly alternate between the notes indicated by continuously hammering on and pulling off.

**TAPPING:** Hammer ("tap") the fret indicated with the pick-hand index or middle finger and pull off to the note fretted by the fret hand.

69

**NATURAL HARMONIC:** Strike the note while the fret-hand lightly touches the string directly over the fret indicated.

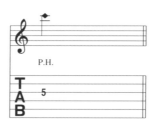

**PINCH HARMONIC:** The note is fretted normally and a harmonic is produced by adding the edge of the thumb or the tip of the index finger of the pick hand to the normal pick attack.

**HARP HARMONIC:** The note is fretted normally and a harmonic is produced by gently resting the pick hand's index finger directly above the indicated fret (in parentheses) while the pick hand's thumb or pick assists by plucking the appropriate string.

**PICK SCRAPE:** The edge of the pick is rubbed down (or up) the string, producing a scratchy sound.

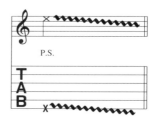

**MUFFLED STRINGS:** A percussive sound is produced by laying the fret hand across the string(s) without depressing, and striking them with the pick hand.

**PALM MUTING:** The note is partially muted by the pick hand lightly touching the string(s) just before the bridge.

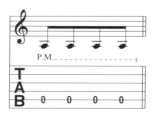

**RAKE:** Drag the pick across the strings indicated with a single motion.

**TREMOLO PICKING:** The note is picked as rapidly and continuously as possible.

**ARPEGGIATE:** Play the notes of the chord indicated by quickly rolling them from bottom to top.

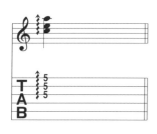

**VIBRATO BAR DIVE AND RETURN:** The pitch of the note or chord is dropped a specified number of steps (in rhythm) then returned to the original pitch.

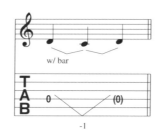

**VIBRATO BAR SCOOP:** Depress the bar just before striking the note, then quickly release the bar.

**VIBRATO BAR DIP:** Strike the note and then immediately drop a specified number of steps, then release back to the original pitch.

# ADDITIONAL MUSICAL DEFINITIONS

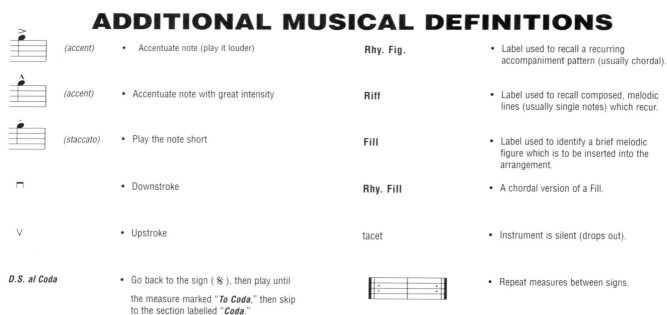

| | | |
|---|---|---|
| (accent) | • Accentuate note (play it louder) | |
| (accent) | • Accentuate note with great intensity | |
| (staccato) | • Play the note short | |
| ⊓ | • Downstroke | |
| V | • Upstroke | |
| *D.S. al Coda* | • Go back to the sign ( 𝄋 ), then play until the measure marked "*To Coda*," then skip to the section labelled "*Coda*." | |
| *D.S. al Fine* | • Go back to the beginning of the song and play until the measure marked "*Fine*" (end). | |

**Rhy. Fig.** — • Label used to recall a recurring accompaniment pattern (usually chordal).

**Riff** — • Label used to recall composed, melodic lines (usually single notes) which recur.

**Fill** — • Label used to identify a brief melodic figure which is to be inserted into the arrangement.

**Rhy. Fill** — • A chordal version of a Fill.

**tacet** — • Instrument is silent (drops out).

• Repeat measures between signs.

• When a repeated section has different endings, play the first ending only the first time and the second ending only the second time.

**NOTE:** Tablature numbers in parentheses mean:
1. The note is being sustained over a system (note in standard notation is tied), or
2. The note is sustained, but a new articulation (such as a hammer-on, pull-off, slide or vibrato begins, or
3. The note is a barely audible "ghost" note (note in standard notation is also in parentheses).

# RECORDED VERSIONS
## *The Best Note-For-Note Transcriptions Available*

**ALL BOOKS INCLUDE TABLATURE**

| | | |
|---|---|---|
| 00694909 Aerosmith – Get A Grip ...............$19.95 | 00660099 Jimi Hendrix – Radio One .............$24.95 | 00690055 Red Hot Chili Peppers – |
| 00690199 Aerosmith – Nine Lives ...............$19.95 | 00690280 Jimi Hendrix – South Saturn Delta ......$19.95 | Bloodsugarsexmagik ................$19.95 |
| 00690146 Aerosmith – Toys in the Attic ..........$19.95 | 00694919 Jimi Hendrix – Stone Free ...........$19.95 | 00690090 Red Hot Chili Peppers – One Hot Minute .$22.95 |
| 00694865 Alice In Chains – Dirt ...............$19.95 | 00690038 Gary Hoey – Best Of ...............$19.95 | 00694892 Guitar Style Of Jerry Reed .............$19.95 |
| 00660225 Alice In Chains – Facelift .............$19.95 | 00660029 Buddy Holly ....................$19.95 | 00694937 Jimmy Reed – Master Bluesman .......$19.95 |
| 00694925 Alice In Chains – Jar Of Flies/Sap ......$19.95 | 00660169 John Lee Hooker – A Blues Legend .....$19.95 | 00694899 R.E.M. – Automatic For The People .....$19.95 |
| 00694932 Allman Brothers Band – Volume 1 .....$24.95 | 00690054 Hootie & The Blowfish – | 00694898 R.E.M. – Out Of Time ...............$19.95 |
| 00694933 Allman Brothers Band – Volume 2 .....$24.95 | Cracked Rear View .................$19.95 | 00690014 Rolling Stones – Exile On Main Street ...$24.95 |
| 00694934 Allman Brothers Band – Volume 3 .....$24.95 | 00690143 Hootie & The Blowfish – | 00690186 Rolling Stones – Rock & Roll Circus ...$19.95 |
| 00694877 Chet Atkins – Guitars For All Seasons ...$19.95 | Fairweather Johnson ...............$19.95 | 00690135 Otis Rush Collection ...............$19.95 |
| 00694918 Randy Bachman Collection ...........$22.95 | 00694905 Howlin' Wolf ....................$19.95 | 00690133 Rusted Root – When I Woke ........$19.95 |
| 00694880 Beatles – Abbey Road ...............$19.95 | 00690136 Indigo Girls – 1200 Curfews .........$22.95 | 00690031 Santana's Greatest Hits ...............$19.95 |
| 00694891 Beatles – Revolver ...............$19.95 | 00694938 Elmore James – | 00694805 Scorpions – Crazy World ...........$19.95 |
| 00694863 Beatles – | Master Electric Slide Guitar ..........$19.95 | 00690150 Son Seals – Bad Axe Blues .........$17.95 |
| Sgt. Pepper's Lonely Hearts Club Band ..$19.95 | 00690167 Skip James Blues Guitar Collection ....$16.95 | 00690128 Seven Mary Three – American Standards .$19.95 |
| 00690174 Beck – Mellow Gold ...............$17.95 | 00694833 Billy Joel For Guitar ...............$19.95 | 00690076 Sex Pistols – Never Mind The Bollocks .$19.95 |
| 00690175 Beck – Odelay ...................$17.95 | 00694912 Eric Johnson – Ah Via Musicom ......$19.95 | 00120105 Kenny Wayne Shepherd – Ledbetter Heights$19.95 |
| 00694931 Belly – Star ....................$19.95 | 00690169 Eric Johnson – Venus Isle ...........$22.95 | 00690196 Silverchair – Freak Show ...........$19.95 |
| 00694884 The Best of George Benson ..........$19.95 | 00694799 Robert Johnson – At The Crossroads .....$19.95 | 00690130 Silverchair – Frogstomp ...........$19.95 |
| 00692385 Chuck Berry ...................$19.95 | 00693185 Judas Priest – Vintage Hits ...........$19.95 | 00690041 Smithereens – Best Of ...............$19.95 |
| 00692200 Black Sabbath – | 00690073 B. B. King – 1950-1957 ...........$24.95 | 00694885 Spin Doctors – Pocket Full Of Kryptonite .$19.95 |
| We Sold Our Soul For Rock 'N' Roll ....$19.95 | 00690098 B. B. King – 1958-1967 ...........$24.95 | 00690124 Sponge – Rotting Pinata ...........$19.95 |
| 00690115 Blind Melon – Soup ...............$19.95 | 00690099 B. B. King – 1962-1971 ...........$24.95 | 00690161 Sponge – Wax Ecstatic .............$19.95 |
| 00690241 Bloodhound Gang – One Fierce Beer Coaster .$19.95 | 00690134 Freddie King Collection ...........$19.95 | 00120004 Steely Dan – Best Of ...............$24.95 |
| 00690028 Blue Oyster Cult – Cult Classics .......$19.95 | 00694903 The Best Of Kiss ...............$24.95 | 00694921 Steppenwolf, The Best Of ...........$22.95 |
| 00690219 Blur .........................$19.95 | 00690157 Kiss – Alive ....................$19.95 | 00694957 Rod Stewart – Acoustic Live .........$22.95 |
| 00690173 Tracy Bonham – The Burdens Of Being Upright $17.95 | 00690163 Mark Knopfler/Chet Atkins – Neck and Neck $19.95 | 00690021 Sting – Fields Of Gold .............$19.95 |
| 00694935 Boston: Double Shot Of .............$22.95 | 00690202 Live – Secret Samadhi .............$19.95 | 00120081 Sublime ......................$19.95 |
| 00690237 Meredith Brooks – Blurring the Edges ...$19.95 | 00690070 Live – Throwing Copper ...........$19.95 | 00690242 Suede – Coming Up ...............$19.95 |
| 00690043 Cheap Trick – Best Of .............$19.95 | 00690018 Living Colour – Best Of ...........$19.95 | 00694824 Best Of James Taylor .............$16.95 |
| 00690171 Chicago – Definitive Guitar Collection ....$22.95 | 00694954 Lynyrd Skynyrd, New Best Of .......$19.95 | 00694887 Thin Lizzy – The Best Of Thin Lizzy ...$19.95 |
| 00690010 Eric Clapton – From The Cradle ......$19.95 | 00694845 Yngwie Malmsteen – Fire And Ice ......$19.95 | 00690238 Third Eye Blind ...............$19.95 |
| 00660139 Eric Clapton – Journeyman .........$19.95 | 00694956 Bob Marley – Legend .............$19.95 | 00690022 Richard Thompson Guitar ...........$19.95 |
| 00694869 Eric Clapton – Live Acoustic .........$19.95 | 00690239 Matchbox 20 – Yourself or Someone Like You .$19.95 | 00690267 311 .........................$19.95 |
| 00694873 Eric Clapton – Timepieces ...........$19.95 | 00690020 Meat Loaf – Bat Out Of Hell I & II .....$22.95 | 00690030 Toad The Wet Sprocket ...........$19.95 |
| 00694896 John Mayall/Eric Clapton – Bluesbreakers $19.95 | 00690244 Megadeath – Cryptic Writings .......$19.95 | 00690228 Tonic – Lemon Parade .............$19.95 |
| 00694940 Counting Crows – August & Everything After $19.95 | 00690011 Megadeath – Youthanasia .........$19.95 | 00694411 U2 – The Joshua Tree .............$19.95 |
| 00690197 Counting Crows – Recovering the Satellites .$19.95 | 00690236 Mighty Mighty Bosstones – Let's Face It ...$19.95 | 00690039 Steve Vai – Alien Love Secrets .........$24.95 |
| 00690118 Cranberries – The Best of .............$19.95 | 00690040 Steve Miller Band Greatest Hits .......$19.95 | 00690172 Steve Vai – Fire Garden .............$24.95 |
| 00694941 Crash Test Dummies – God Shuffled His Feet $19.95 | 00690225 Moist – Creature ...............$19.95 | 00660137 Steve Vai – Passion & Warfare .......$24.95 |
| 00694840 Cream – Disraeli Gears .............$19.95 | 00694802 Gary Moore – Still Got The Blues .....$19.95 | 00690023 Jimmie Vaughan – Strange Pleasures ...$19.95 |
| 00690007 Danzig 4 ......................$19.95 | 00690103 Alanis Morissette – Jagged Little Pill ....$19.95 | 00660136 Stevie Ray Vaughan – In Step .......$19.95 |
| 00690184 DC Talk – Jesus Freak .............$19.95 | 00694958 Mountain, Best Of ...............$19.95 | 00694835 Stevie Ray Vaughan – The Sky Is Crying .$19.95 |
| 00660186 Alex De Grassi Guitar Collection ......$19.95 | 00694895 Nirvana – Bleach ...............$19.95 | 00690015 Stevie Ray Vaughan – Texas Flood ......$19.95 |
| 00694831 Derek And The Dominos – | 00694913 Nirvana – In Utero ...............$19.95 | 00694776 Vaughan Brothers – Family Style ......$19.95 |
| Layla & Other Assorted Love Songs ....$19.95 | 00694883 Nirvana – Nevermind .............$19.95 | 00690217 Verve Pipe, The – Villains .........$19.95 |
| 00690187 Dire Straits – Brothers In Arms .......$19.95 | 00690026 Nirvana – Acoustic In New York ......$19.95 | 00120026 Joe Walsh – Look What I Did... .......$24.95 |
| 00690191 Dire Straits – Money For Nothing ......$24.95 | 00120112 No Doubt – Tragic Kingdom .........$22.95 | 00694789 Muddy Waters – Deep Blues .........$24.95 |
| 00690182 Dishwalla – Pet Your Friends .........$19.95 | 00690273 Oasis – Be Here Now .............$19.95 | 00690071 Weezer ......................$19.95 |
| 00660178 Willie Dixon – Master Blues Composer ...$24.95 | 00690159 Oasis – Definitely Maybe ...........$19.95 | 00690286 Weezer – Pinkerton ...............$19.95 |
| 00690089 Foo Fighters ...................$19.95 | 00690121 Oasis – (What's The Story) Morning Glory $19.95 | 00694970 Who, The – Definitive Collection A-E ....$24.95 |
| 00690042 Robben Ford Blues Collection .........$19.95 | 00690204 Offspring, The – Ixnay on the Hombre ...$17.95 | 00694971 Who, The – Definitive Collection F-Li ...$24.95 |
| 00694920 Free – Best Of ...................$18.95 | 00690203 Offspring, The – Smash .............$17.95 | 00694972 Who, The – Definitive Collection Lo-R ...$24.95 |
| 00690222 G3 Live – Satriani, Vai, Johnson .......$22.95 | 00694830 Ozzy Osbourne – No More Tears ......$19.95 | 00694973 Who, The – Definitive Collection S-Y ....$24.95 |
| 00694894 Frank Gambale – The Great Explorers ...$19.95 | 00694855 Pearl Jam – Ten ...............$19.95 | |
| 00694807 Danny Gatton – 88 Elmira St .........$19.95 | 00690053 Liz Phair – Whip Smart .............$19.95 | |
| 00690127 Goo Goo Dolls – A Boy Named Goo ......$19.95 | 00690176 Phish – Billy Breathes .............$22.95 | |
| 00690117 John Gorka Collection ...............$19.95 | 00690240 Phish – Hoist ...................$19.95 | |
| 00690114 Buddy Guy Collection Vol. A-J .......$19.95 | 00693800 Pink Floyd – Early Classics .........$19.95 | |
| 00690193 Buddy Guy Collection Vol. L-Y .......$19.95 | 00694967 Police – Message In A Box Boxed Set ...$70.00 | |
| 00694798 George Harrison Anthology .........$19.95 | 00690125 Presidents of the United States of America .$19.95 | |
| 00690068 Return Of The Hellecasters ...........$19.95 | 00690195 Presidents of the United States of America II $22.95 | |
| 00692930 Jimi Hendrix – Are You Experienced? ...$19.95 | 00694974 Queen – A Night At The Opera .......$19.95 | |
| 00692931 Jimi Hendrix – Axis: Bold As Love ......$19.95 | 00694910 Rage Against The Machine ...........$19.95 | |
| 00660192 The Jimi Hendrix – Concerts .........$24.95 | 00690145 Rage Against The Machine – Evil Empire ..$19.95 | |
| 00692932 Jimi Hendrix – Electric Ladyland .......$24.95 | 00690179 Rancid – And Out Come the Wolves ....$22.95 | |
| 00690218 Jimi Hendrix – First Rays of the New Rising Sun $24.95 | | |

# GUITAR *signature licks*

The Signature Licks book/audio packs are especially formatted to give you instruction on how to play a particular artist style by using the actual transcribed, "right from the record" licks! Designed for use by anyone from beginner right up to the experienced player who is looking to expand his insight. The books contain full performance notes and an overview of each artist or group's style with transcriptions in notes and tab. The audio features playing tips and techniques as well as playing examples at a slower tempo.

### Acoustic Guitar Of '60s And '70s
*by Wolf Marshall*
A step-by-step breakdown of acoustic guitar styles and techniques featuring 14 classic rock examples, including: Here Comes The Sun • Fire And Rain • Dust In The Wind • Babe, I'm Gonna Leave You • Angie • and more.

00695024  Book/CD Pack....................................$19.95

### Acoustic Guitar Of '80s And '90s
*by Wolf Marshall*
Learn to play acoustic guitar in the styles and techniques of today's top performers. This book/CD pack features detailed instruction on 15 examples, including: Tears In Heaven • Patience • Losing My Religion • Wanted Dead Or Alive • and more.

00695033  Book/CD Pack....................................$19.95

### The Best Of Eric Clapton
*by Jeff Perrin*
A step-by-step breakdown of his playing technique through a hands-on analysis of classics. Includes: After Midnight • Crossroads • Layla • Tears In Heaven • Wonderful Tonight • and more.

00695038  Book/CD Pack....................................$19.95

### The Best Of Def Leppard
A step-by-step breakdown of the band's guitar styles and techniques featuring songs from four albums. The audio accompaniment presents each song in a stereo split with full band backing. Songs include: Bringin' On The Heartbreak • Hysteria • Photograph • and more.

00696516  Book/CD Pack....................................$19.95

### Jimi Hendrix
12 songs presented with all of the guitar parts fully transcribed, plus accompanying audio on CD, as performed by a full band. A performance notes, outlining chord voicings, scale use, and unusual techniques are including for each song. Songs include: Foxy Lady • Hey Joe • Little Wing • Purple Haze • and more.

00696560  Book/CD Pack....................................$19.95

### Eric Johnson
Learn the nuances of technique and taste that make Eric Johnson unique among guitarists. On this pack's 60-minute audio supplement, Wolf Marshall explores both the theoretical and hands-on aspects of Eric Johnson's best recorded work. It also comprehensively explores: Hybrid picking • String-skipping • Motivic development • Scale-combining • Position shifting • and additional aspects of his playing that makes him one of the most admired guitarists today. Some of his best songs are examined, including: Trademark • Cliffs Of Dover • Song For George • and more.
00699317  Book/CD Pack .................................$19.95
00699318  Book/Cassette Pack...........................$17.95

### The Best Of Kiss
Learn the trademark riffs and solos behind one of rock's most legendary bands. This pack includes a hands-on analysis of 12 power house classics, including: Deuce • Strutter • Rock And Roll All Nite • Detroit Rock City • and more.

00699412  Book/Cassette Pack ........................$17.95
00699413  Book/CD Pack ................................$19.95

### The Guitars Of Elvis
*by Wolf Marshall*
Elvis' music is synonymous with the birth of rock and roll and the invention of rock guitar. Wolf Marshall takes you back to the roots where it all started with this exploration into the influential style of the King's fretmen. This book is a step-by-step breakdown of the playing techniques of Scotty Moore, Hank Garland, and James Burton. Players will learn their unique concepts and techniques by studying this special collection of Elvis' greatest guitar-driven moments. The 75-minute accompanying audio presents each song in stereo-split with full band backing. Songs include: A Big Hunk O' Love • Heartbreak Hotel • Hound Dog • Jailhouse Rock • See See Rider • and more!
00696508  Book/Cassette Pack...........................$17.95
00696507  Book/CD Pack ..................................$19.95

### Rolling Stones
*by Wolf Marshall*
A step-by-step breakdown of the guitar styles of Keith Richards, Brian Jones, Mick Taylor and Ron Wood. 17 songs are explored, including: Beast Of Burden • It's Only Rock 'n' Roll (But I Like It) • Not Fade Away • Start Me Up • Tumbling Dice • and more.

00695079  Book/CD Pack................................$19.95

### Best Of Carlos Santana
Explore the music behind one of the guitar's greatest innovators. A Hands-on analysis of 13 classics, including Black Magic Woman • Evil Ways • Oye Como Va • Song Of The Wind • and more.

00695010  Book/CD Pack ................................$19.95

### Steve Vai
Play along with the actual backing tracks from *Passion and Warfare* and *Sex and Religion* especially modified by Steve Vai himself! Learn the secrets behind a guitar virtuoso then play along like the pro himself.

00673247  Book/CD Pack................................$22.95

### Stevie Ray Vaughan
*by Wolf Marshall*
This book takes you on an in-depth exploration of this guitar genius by examining various aspects of Vaughan's playing. Marshall explains his influences, tuning, equipment, picking technique and other aspects of Vaughan's sound. In addition, he transcribes, in notes and tab, parts of 13 of Vaughan's most famous songs, and explains how they were played and what makes them so unique. The 59-minute accompanying cassette or CD includes samples of the parts of the songs being examined. A must for any serious Vaughan fan or aspiring guitarist!
00699315  Book/Cassette Pack...........................$17.95
00699316  Book/CD Pack .................................$19.95

Prices, contents, and availability subject to change without notice. Some products may not be available outside the U.S.A.

FOR MORE INFORMATION, SEE YOUR LOCAL MUSIC DEALER, OR WRITE TO:

# HAL•LEONARD
CORPORATION™
7777 W. BLUEMOUND RD. P.O. BOX 13819 MILWAUKEE, WI 53213

**http://www.halleonard.com**

0298